THE

DESCENT

OF THE SUN

THE

DESCENT

OF THE SUN

(चिविक्रमाधोगांश्री:)

A CYCLE OF BIRTH

TRANSLATED FROM THE ORIGINAL MANUSCRIPT

by

F.W. BAIN

[1903]

ज्ञाग्रत्स्वप्रपंचदर्शनम्

(The illusion of a waking dream.)

Like a Digit of the Moon
In the Shadow of the Earth
Spirit undergoeth Swoon
In the Vestibule of Birth:
Dreameth transitory Trouble,
Weareth Hues of Heaven, hurled
Hither, thither, as a Bubble
On the Ocean of the World.

स्वप्ने ततो मया दृष्टं नमदच्युतमम्बुजम्

'and in a dream I saw a lotus fallen from heaven'

Dedicated to Margaret

INTRODUCTION

HERE is a fairy tale which I found in an old Hindu manuscript.

As the title shows, it is a solar myth. Literally translated, its name
is: *The glory of the Going Down of the Sun*. But this is only the
exoteric, physical envelope of the inner, mystical meaning, which
is: *The Divine Lustre[1] of the Descent (Incarnation) of Him Who
took Three Steps*: i.e. Vishnu, or the Sun, the later Krishna, or
Hindu Apollo. And this epithet of the Sun is explained by the
well-known passage in the Rig-Veda (I. 22. 17[2]), '*Three steps did
Vishnu stride: thrice did he set down his foot*.' A mythological
expression for the rise, the zenith, and the set of the Sun. But the
old magnificent simplicity of the Rig-Veda was perverted by
subsequent Pauranik glosses; and Vishnu, according to the new
legend, was said to have cheated his adversary, Bali, by striding, in
his Dwarf Incarnation, over the three worlds. In our title, a

---

[1] *Shrí* also means a Sacred Lotus, and it is the name of the twelfth Digit of the
Moon: thus indicating the position of this story in the series to which it
belongs: for an account of which, and the manuscript, I may refer the reader to
the preface to her predecessor *Shashiní*, entitled *A Digit of the Moon*.
[2] Cp. also I. 154, 155, and elsewhere. It should be observed that learned
doctors differ as to the interpretation of the *three strides*: but this is not the
place to examine their views.

9

different turn is given to the old idea, which we may express by saying that the steps commence, not with the rise, but the set of the Sun: his Going Down, his mysterious period of Darkness, his Rising again. This is the inverted Race, or Cycle of the Sun, which so much exercised the mind of primitive man, and seemed to be a symbol of the mystery of Birth and Death.

And ours is a strange story; which seemed to the translator not unworthy of being clothed in an English dress, containing as it did so much in little bulk that, as the French say, *donne à penser.* Absolutely Hindu in its form and spirit, it is for an Englishman full of associations, and instinct with that philosophical mythology, scraps and fragments of which are familiar to him in the story of the Fall and the poetry of Milton, in many an old fairy tale, in some touches of Pythagoras and Plato, and some old religious legends. *Lux in tenebris:* a dazzling light, in the most profound darkness: the night of the sun: a heavenly body, doomed to put on mortality and suffer for a period in this lower world of darkness, birth and death: in some such ways as these we may express its central idea. But for the reader not acquainted with Sanskrit it may be worth while to point out that there runs throughout it a veiled allegory which he would not be apt to detect, to the teaching of the Sánkhya Philosophy of Kapila, (who is older than Thales;) according to which it is the duty of PURUSHA, the archetype of the spirit of man, the Primæval Male, to hunt for and pursue PRAKRITI, the feminine personification of material Nature, the Eternal Feminine, till he finds her: when instantly she disappears 'like an actress[3].' In this respect, the story somewhat recalls the *Gita-Gowind* of Jayadewa, which according to one school of interpreters, deals with the Soul, personified as the lovely Rádhá, in its search after the Divine. For

---

[3] From this point of view, the period of Night would be the reign of *Tamas,* one of the three great categories of that philosophy: the Quality of *Darkness,* as opposed to *Light, Ignorance,* as opposed to *Knowledge, Evil,* as opposed to *Good,* the World *Below,* as opposed to the World *Above.*

among the Hindus, the earthly and the heavenly love are always confounded.

And let not anyone suppose, that the lesson embodied to these pages is obsolete or dead in the India of to-day. I wrote the last lines of this translation late one evening, and I walked out in the dusk to the bridge across the river, about half a mile away. There was not a breath of air. It was a night as still as that which long ago Medea chose on which to work her spells: nothing moved save the twinkling stars; all below was plunged in sleep, every tree a picture, every leaf seemed carved in stone: only, every now and then, a flying fox burst screeching from a branch. And as I stood upon the bridge, I could hear a faint din of tom-toms coming from the distant city of the Peshwas. I looked westwards, up the river. The sun had set, leaving behind it a ruddy glare which faded higher up the sky into the darkness: and exactly on the confines of the colours, in that bath of *nilalohita*, that *purple-red*, which is a favourite epithet of the god Shiwa, hung, like a thing in a dream, the lovely streak of the new moon, one day old. All was reflected in the still mirror of the broad sheet of water formed by the river *Bund*, or dam.

I turned round. On the eastern side, below the bridge, the river runs in disconnected pools. All was buried in dark and gloom. But about two hundred yards away, on the right bank, there was a red spot and leaping flames. They were burning on the bank a corpse, whose former owner had died of plague. For here in Poona it is now, as it was of old in the days of Homer, αἰεὶ δὲ πυραὶ νεκύων καίοντο θαμειαί. . . .

Suddenly a voice said behind me: They burn well on a cold night. I looked round. Beside me stood a Hindu, whose real name I do not think it lawful to mention. His white clothes were stained and splashed all over with red, for the Holi festival had left its mark on him.

11

Why, Wishwanáth, I said, what are you doing here?

Or have you come, like me, merely *dekhne ke wáste*, to see the sun set, and 'eat air'?

Wishwanáth cast a careless glance at the sky. Yes, he said, it looks well from here: but then I have seen it so often. It was a new moon yesterday.

And very soon it will be old. Look, Wishwanáth, here is a strange thing. See, there on that side is the moon, following the sun to rest in a bath of fire, and they will both appear to-morrow all the better for it. But now, look down there. There is another thing passing, away in the fire. But how will it be with *that*?

And I pointed to the burning pyre on the other side.

The Hindu looked steadily at it for a moment, and then at me. It will be just the same, he said.

What! you think that *that* will come back again, like sun and moon?

He did not answer for a moment. Then he said slowly, in a low voice, as if speaking rather to himself than me: How should it not return? *na jáyate mriyate wa kadáchit*[4].

I looked at him, but said nothing. He continued to gaze steadily at the burning pyre, in silence, and I did the same. The flames were dying down: their work was done.

Metempsychosis, transmigration, everlasting incarnation and re-incarnation of the immortal soul in body after body, birth after birth: all Hindu literature is but the kaleidoscopic reiteration of

---

[4] From the Bhagwad-Gítá: IT *is never born and never dies.*

this one identical idea, whose beauty is such that no logic will ever destroy it or oust it in favour of another. For the Sanskrit language is a kind of shrine, consecrated to the embodiment and immortalisation of this philosophical myth. The Hindus are possessed by it; it is their hereditary heirloom, *Kramágatam*, the legacy from an immemorial past: it is all that they have left. And nations, like the characters in our story, cling desperately, in periods of degradation and eclipse, to all that reminds them of a former state of ideal prosperity, which lingers in their literature and echoes in their souls, like dim recollections of a forgotten paradise, or faint reminiscences of a former birth. Distance lends enchantment, and time effaces detail, and endows stern realities with dreamy beauty; and thus a rugged stony past fades gradually into a picture, blue, soft, and unutterably beautiful, like some low barren island, seen far away in the haze, over a hot and glittering sea.

POONA,
March 25, 1903.

13

CONTENTS

Note.--As the story belongs, by its title, both to Sun and Moon, it should be observed, that the Night and the two Twilights, Dusk and Dawn, apply to both in opposite ways. The Moon rises when the Sun sets, reigns over the Night when he is buried in Darkness, and either sets or vanishes when he is risen in his light. For the Moon is the type of Night, or this lower world (ihaloka), but the Sun, of Day, that is, of the other.

SUNSET

AN EVIL EYE.

The Descent of the Sun.

INVOCATION.

O glorious and infinite Spirit of Peace, Lord of Ascetics, who whirling round in thy wild dance dost lend as it were its colour to the sky, in whose mirror are seen reflected the blueness of thy throat and the silver digit of the moon in the matted tufts of thy tawny hair: thee we adore. And we worship the ever victorious trunk of the Elephant of Elephants, whose fierce glare consumes the innumerable hosts of opposing obstacles, as a forest fire shrivels the blades of dry grass [5].

LONG ago, on the slopes of Himálaya, there lived a young King of the Spirits of the Air, named Kamalamitra [6]; for he was a portion of the Sun. And he worshipped the husband of Umá[7]. And he turned his back on the pleasures of the senses, and went afar off, and dwelt alone, among the icy peaks and snowy plateaux

---

[5] For Ganésha's trunk is usually smeared with vermilion. The other deity is, of course, Shiva.

[6] '*The lover of the lotus,*' i.e. the Sun. *Mitra* is also one of his names. [*Kam*- rhymes with *drum.*]

[7] i.e. Shiwa. Umá is his wife.

that lie around Kailás. And there he remained, living at first upon leaves, and then upon smoke, and finally upon air, performing penances of appalling severity, till after a hundred years[8] that Lord of Creatures was moved to compassion. And he appeared to him, in the twilight of evening, in the guise of an ascetic, but in stature like a tall tree, with the new moon in his hair, and said: I am pleased with thy devotion, so now I grant thee a boon: ask. Then the young King bowed before him, and said: Blessed One, let me continue in this contemplation of thee: that is enough. Then said Maheshwara: This is well said: nevertheless, ask of me some boon. Then said Kamalamitra: Since it is so, and I must absolutely choose, then give me a wife, whose eyes, like these hills and this sky, shall be full of the dusky lustre[9] of thy throat and thy moon, as if, insatiate of gazing at thee, they had become, not transitory mirrors, but pictures permanently stained with thy glory. For so shall she be a medium of devotion between me and thee.

Then the moon-crested God was pleased. But he looked into the future, by his magic power of divination, and saw what was coming. And he said slowly: Eyes such as these will be dangerous, not only to others, but also to their owner. Nevertheless, I have given thee a boon: thou shalt have thy desire.

Then he disappeared, and Kamalamitra returned home rejoicing. And by the favour of the deity all the emaciation and fatigue of his penances left him, and he became strong as Bhima and beautiful as Arjuna[10]. And he arrived at his palace on the evening of the next day, and went into the garden to repose, as the sun was going down. And as he went, he looked before him, and

---

[8] This is a sort of Hindu *façon de parler*: it must not be supposed to make him any the older.

[9] *nila*. As this colour is the keynote of the story, it should be observed, that it is a deep, intense blue, inclining to black, essentially associated in Hindu literature with the moon-crested God, peacocks, and the lotus.

[10] Characters in the Mahábhárata.

suddenly he saw a woman, floating on a pool of white lotuses, in a boat of sandal, with silver oars. And her glances fell on those snowy flowers, and turned their tint to blue, for her eyes were lowered, and she was resting her chin on one hand as she lay, and with the other dropping one by one into the water the petals of a lotus red as blood. And the round curve of her hip stood up like a sand bank, and was mirrored again in the silent water below. And her lips moved, for she was counting the petals as they fell.

And Kamalamitra stood still, holding his breath, and gazing at her, fearing to move, for he thought it was a dream. Then all at once she looked up and saw him, and smiled, bathing him with the colour of her eyes. And it seemed to Kamalamitra that he stood in a pool of colour formed by the essence of all the blue lotuses in the world. And then suddenly he remembered the boon of the God who is clothed with heaven[11], and he exclaimed: Surely thou art my own wife, sent me by the God who keeps his promises, and none other. For yesterday I gazed at his glory, and now I am gazing at thy two eyes, and it is the same. And if it be so, by what name shall I call thee? Then she said: My name is Anushayiní[12], and for what purpose did the Creator form these eyes, but to reflect the image of their lord?

Then Kamalamitra, having thus obtained her from the deity, took possession of his lovely little wife, and thereafter remained with her in the region about Kailás, utterly bewildered and intoxicated by constantly gazing at those mirrors of deity, her two great eyes. And he plunged into their sea, and was drowned in it, and the whole world seemed to him to be made of lotus blue[13]. And like a vessel filled to the brim and running over, he was so overflowing

---

[11] *digambara.*

[12] '*a devoted wife.*' But the word has another technical philosophical significance: it connotes evil, clinging to the soul by reason of sin in a former birth, and begetting the necessity of expiation in another body.

[13] *Kuwalayamayamjagat.* When I was young, sings Bhartrihari, the whole world seemed to me to be made of woman (*nárimayam*)

with delight in her beauty, and the pride of having so unique a specimen of womankind all to himself, that he could not contain his emotion, but sought relief in going about everywhere talking about her, and trying to get everybody to acknowledge, what he thought himself, that all other women in the world were absolutely nothing in comparison with his own wife. Alas! a woman is one thing, and emancipation quite another.

So it happened, that on a day, when he was disputing about her with one of his friends, and abusing him, for not readily admitting all his own eulogies of his wife, that friend of his suddenly burst out laughing, and exclaimed: For all things there is a cure, even for snake-bite there is a cure, but there is no cure, for one who has been bitten with a woman's beauty. Know, O thou infatuated lover, that the golden glamour of our Other Half, Man's ectype, Woman, is not like a simple musical theme, but one infinitely various, containing ten thousand notes, and stirring like a churning stick all the emotions in the ocean of the soul of man. And however beautiful may be thy wife's eyes, still eyes are only eyes, and a woman is not all eye, but something more. For one woman witches us, like a waterfall, with the music of her bubbling laughter, and another entrances us, like a forest-pool, with the peace of her shadowy silence. And one entangles us, like Yama[14], in the nectar-nooses of her hair, while another pierces us, like Manobhawa[15], with the archery of her poisoned eyes. And one enflames us, like the Sun, in the fever-fire of sick desire, while another soothes us, like the Moon, by the camphor of her dewy kisses. And like oxen, we are goaded, by the biting sting of one woman's evil, and like elephants, we are tamed, by the subtle spell of another's purity; and like birds, we are decoyed, by the lure of the bower of one girl's arms, and like bees, we hover and sip, around the honey of another's lips, and like snakes, we wind and

---

[14] Death, who is represented with a noose (*pásha*).
[15] Love, whose weapon is his bow.

coil[16] round the slender stem of one girl's waist, and like weary travellers, we long to sleep on the living pillow of another's bosom. Then Kamalamitra broke in impatiently: Away with the fascinations, of all the women in the three worlds, past, present, or to come! Could they unite to form the very body of the god of love, yet the eyes of Anushayiní, alone, would, like the eye of the enemy of Kaudarpa[17], reduce them to ashes. Aye! those eyes, with their blue irresistible invitation, would succeed in corrupting sages, where Menaká, Tilottamá[18] and the rest had failed.

Then his friend laughed in derision, and said: Boasting is useless, and in words, all men can do everything, and every woman is another Rambhá[19]. Babble no more of her beauty, but come, let your paragon of a wife put her power to the proof. For hard by here, in the wood on the hillside, is an aged Sage, named Pápanáshana[20], whose austerities terrify even the gods. He would be an admirable touchstone for the eyes of this wonderful wife of yours, whose beauty exists, like a bubble, only on the stream of your words.

And then, stung by the taunt, Kamalamitra exclaimed in wrath: Fool! if she does not turn him from his asceticism as easily as amber draws after it stubble and grass, I will cut off my own head and cast it into the Ganges. Then his friend laughed again, and said: Do nothing rash, thou art not Daksha[21]: once gone, thy head

---

[16] There is here an untranslateable play on the word *bhoga*: which means both the coil of a snake and enjoyment.

[17] Alluding to the legend that Shiva annihilated the god of love, who was endeavoring to inflame him, by a fiery glance from his third eye. Love's sacred fire met in this case, for once, with an element more potent than his own.

[18] The legend of S. Antony is but a western echo of the stories of these nymphs, whom the jealous gods employed as weapons to destroy the virtue of sages whose accumulated asceticism was becoming *mountainous* and dangerous. Like the Devil, and long before him, they baited the hook with a pretty woman.

[19] See the Rámayan, book I.

[20] '*destroyer of guilt.*'

[21] Whose true head was cut off and replaced by that of a ram.

can never be restored. But Kamalamitra hurried away to find Anushayiní. And he found her in the garden by the lotus pool, and told her of his brag, and said: Come instantly, and make the experiment, and vindicate the power of those wonderful eyes of thine, and my own faith in them, without delay. For I burn to convict that foolish sceptic of his folly, by ocular demonstration.

Then Anushayiní said slowly: Dear husband, thou wert angry, and therefore indiscreet, and I fear, lest by doing evil we may bring on ourselves punishment. For expiation follows guilt, as surely as Orion treads on the heels of Rohini[22] There is sin and danger in this rash experiment. And now it will be better for us not to venture upon the verge of a precipice, over which we may both fall, into irreparable disaster.

But as she spoke, her eyes rested on Kamalamitra, and bewildered him, and destroyed the persuasion of her words. For he heard nothing that she said, but was full of the blindness of passion, and more than ever convinced of the omnipotence of her beauty. And so, seeing that she could not turn him from his will, Anushayiní gave in, and yielded , to him as to her deity. Nay, in the interior of her heart she rejoiced, to find that she could not dissuade him, for she was filled with curiosity herself; to see whether in truth her beauty would prevail over the ascetic, though she trembled for the consequences. Alas, where beauty, and curiosity, and youth, and self-will, and intoxication combine, like a mad elephant, where is the cotton thread of self-control?

Then those two lovers kissed each other passionately, like travellers who have been separated for a year. And yet they knew not that they were doing so for the last time. And then they went together to the forest, to find that old ascetic. And hand-in-hand they rambled about, like a pair of Love's arrows in human form[23],

---

[22] An astronomical simile: the ninth and tenth signs of the lunar zodiac.
[23] They were not human, but semi-divine; still, it is impossible to express the idea of incarnation except in terms of humanity.

till they penetrated to the very heart of that wood. And there on a sudden they came upon that old sage, and saw him standing, plunged in meditation, motionless as a tree. And round him the ants had built up their hills, and his beard and hair trailed from his head, like creepers, and ran down along the ground, and were covered with leaves: and over his withered limbs played a pair of lizards, like living emeralds. And he looked straight before him, with great eyes that mirrored everything, but saw nothing, clear and unfathomable and still, like mountain tarns in which all the fish are asleep.

And Kamalamitra and Anushayiní looked at him awhile in silence, and then at each other, and trembled, for they knew that they were staking their souls. But as he wavered, the thought of his friend's derision came back into Kamalamitra's mind, and filled him with anger. And he said to Anushayiní: Advance, and let this old *muni*[24] see you, and I will mark the result.

So Anushayiní went forward, obeying his command, and stepped over the leaves with feet lighter than themselves, till she stood in front of the sage. And when she saw that he did not move, she raised herself on tiptoe to look into his eyes, saying to herself: Possibly he is dead. And she looked into those eyes, and saw there nothing save two images of herself; like two incarnations of timidity, that seemed to say to her as it were: Beware! And as she stood there, trembling in the swing of uncertainty, Kamalamitra watched her with ecstasy and laughed to himself; and said: Certainly that old *muni* is no longer alive, for otherwise she would have reached his soul through the door of his eyes, were it down in the lower world.

So as they stood there, waiting, gradually that old sage came to himself: for he felt that his meditations were being disturbed by something or other. And he looked, and saw Anushayiní standing

[24] *man of silence,*' which, according to Kalidas and Bhartrihari, is the golden rule whether for fools or sages.

before him like the new moon at the close of day, a pure form of exquisite beauty[25], a crystal without a flaw, tinged with the colour of heaven. And instantly, by the power of his own mystical meditation, he divined the whole truth, and the exact state of the case. And he cast at that wayward beauty a glance, sorrowful as that of a deer, yet terrible as a thunderbolt: and immediately courage fled from her soul, and strength from her knees, and she sank to the ground with drooping head, like a lotus broken by the wind.

But Kamalamitra rushed forward, and caught her in his arms. Then as they stood together, the old ascetic spoke and cursed them, saying slowly: Irreverent lovers, now shall that beauty which occasioned this insolence meet with its appropriate reward. Descend now, ye guilty ones, into mortal wombs, and suffer in the lower world the pangs of separation, till ye have purged away your guilt in the fire of human sorrow.

Then hearing the doom of separation, wild with grief they fell at his feet, and implored him, saying: Fix at least a term to the curse, and a period to our pain. And he said again: When one of you shall slay the other, the curse shall end.

Then those two unhappy lovers looked at each other in mute despair. And they drew in that instant from each other's eyes a deep draught of the nectar of mutual contemplation, as if to sustain them in their pilgrimage over the terrible sea of separation, saying as it were to each other, but in vain[26]: Remember me! Then all of a sudden they disappeared and went, like flashes of lightning, somewhere else.

---

[25] *Sushamásheshá*: an incomparable expression, meaning, as applied to the thin streak of the new moon at dusk, that everything of it was gone, except its beauty: *venustas, et præterea nihil!*

[26] Because the former birth is always forgotten. But see the sequel.

But Maheshwara, from his seat on Kailás, saw them go, for as fate would have it, he chanced to be looking in that direction. And grasping the whole truth by mystical intuition [27], he remembered his boon to the Spirit of the Air, and he said to himself: Now has the future which I foresaw become the present[28], and the blue eyes of Anushayiní have produced a catastrophe. But I must not leave her lovely body to the play of chance, for it has in it something of my own divinity. And Kamalamitra, after all, was not very much to blame. For he was bewildered by my glory, reflected in her eyes. So I am the culprit, who is responsible for this state of affairs: and so I must look after this pair of lovers. Moreover, I have a mind to amuse myself with their adventures[29].

So after considering awhile, that Master Yogi took a lotus, and placing it on the earth in a distant sea, it became an island. And he made in it, by his magic power, an earthly copy of a heavenly type, of a nature known to himself alone, for the future to unfold. And having completed his arrangements, he allowed the chain of events to take its course.

But the old sage Pápanáshana, when those two lovers had disappeared, remained in the forest alone. And their images forsook the mirror of his eyes, and faded away from his mind, like the shadow of a cloud travelling over the surface of a great lake, and vanished, and were utterly forgotten.

---

[27] This power of gods and ascetics of a high order, frequently alluded to, reposes upon *yoga*, i.e. intense concentration, which is the secret of Pátanjali. There is a kernel of truth in it, after all.
[28] *Time* is another name of Shiwa.
[29] The whole creation, according to Manu (i. 80) is the sport of the deity.

NIGHT

A SLEEP AND A DREAM

I. A Lotus of the Day

BUT Anushayiní[30], when she disappeared in the forest, fell down
to earth like a falling star, and entered the womb of the favourite
wife of the King of Indirálaya[31], and was born after the manner of
mortals as his daughter. And at that moment she lit up the birth
chamber with the radiance diffused from her body, which put the
lamps to shame. And the nurses and waiting women were
astonished, for wonderful to say! the lids of the child's eyes were
fringed with long black lashes, looking like rain-clouds hanging
low to hide the rising moon. And suddenly those lashes rose like a
curtain, and there came from beneath them a flood of blue colour,
which pervaded the room like the odour of camphor and sandal-
wood made visible to the eye, and overcame the senses of all that
stood by, till they were within a little of swooning away. And like
men lying on their backs and gazing into the depths of the sky,
they felt as it were enveloped in the colour of heaven, and lost

---

[30] That is, her soul, as distinguished from her body: that part of her which,
according to Plato and the Bhagwad-Gítá (more logical than modern
theologians) *is never born* and *never dies.*
[31] *The home of Shrí,* i.e. a blue lotus, which is so called because the goddess
Shrí appeared floating in one at the creation.

26

their perception of mundane affairs. For though they knew it not, they were looking at the reflection of the glory of the moon-crested god.

So they all stood round in silence, watching the child's eyes. And at last, the King, and his ministers, and his physicians and astrologers, drew a long breath, and looked at each other in amazement. And the prime-minister said: King, this is a wonderful thing. For these eyes are the eyes, not of a child, but of a sage[32], or rather, of a god. And surely this is no mere mortal maiden, but rather some deity, or portion of a deity, smitten by a curse, and doomed thereby to descend for a period into this lower world, to expiate awhile sins committed in a former birth. For such things often come about. And beyond a doubt your Majesty is favoured, in being chosen by the deity to be the means of his incarnation. Then hearing this speech of his minister, whose words were always suited to the events, the King was excessively delighted. And he celebrated the birth of his daughter with extraordinary magnificence, and gave gold and villages to Brahmans and the poor. And taking counsel with his astrologers and Brahman sages skilled in names and their applications, he gave to his daughter the auspicious name of Shrí [33]. For he said: Her eyes are like lotuses, and like the pools in which they dwell: and surely they are the very echo of the eyes of the Goddess of Beauty when she rose from the sea, and lay in her blue lotus cradle, lapped by the foam of which she was composed, and gazing at the wondering waves with eyes that mocked them, and robbed them of their hue.

Then time passed away, and the years with the seasons followed each other like caravans over the desert, and old age and grey hair came and took up their dwelling at the wrinkled root of the

---

[32] *shánta*: one who has quelled the passions and attained peace. Of such, Shiwa is the chief. But the minister drew his bow at a venture, and knew not how he hit the mark.
[33] Hence the name of the city, above.

King's ear. And meanwhile Shrí grew from a child into a girl, and at length the dawn of her womanhood broke. And like the horns of the waxing moon, her limbs rounded and swelled into the very perfect orb of supreme loveliness, and she became as it were the very salt of the sea of beauty[34], inspiring in all who drank of it insatiable thirst, and an intolerable craving for the water of the blue lakes of her eyes. And at last there came a day when the King her father looked at her, and said to himself: The fruit is ripe: and now it is time that it were plucked and eaten.

So he went to the apartments of the women, to find her mother, his principal Queen, Madirekshaná[35]. But when she learned the object of his coming, the Queen said: *Aryaputra*[36], it is useless. For our daughter will not even listen to the word husband, much less undergo the thing. The King said: What is this? Should the cornfield refuse the plough, or a maiden refuse to be married? Is she not now of ripe age, and does not a grown-up maiden in the house bring upon herself and her relations infamy in this world and the next? Madirekshaná said: Speak to her yourself, and persuade her to it if you can. For of her own accord she told me, that her marriage was a thing not to be thought of, even in a dream.

So the King sent for his daughter, to question her himself.

And after a while, Shrí came in, undulating as she moved like a swan[37], and swaying like a flower waving in the wind: for her waist could be grasped by the fist, and her bosom was glorious, like the swell of an ocean wave. And like a child she smiled at her

---

[34] Beauty and salt, in the original, are denoted by the same word.
[35] That is, 'a woman with sweet seductive eyes.'
[36] A pretty term employed by ladies in addressing their lords: 'son of an *arya*, a gentleman.' It has no English equivalent.
[37] The old Hindus had a special admiration and a special term (*hansagamini*) for a woman who walked like a swan.

father[38] with parted lips and half-shut eyes, casting before her through the net of their lashes the magical charm of the colour of a wet lotus: and her girdle jingled as if with joy, while the flashing jewels with which she was covered all over changed colour, as if with envy at being outshone by the play[39] of her eyes. And the old King looked at her with pride and wonder and delight: and he laughed to himself, and said: Wonderful is the cunning of the Creator, and incomprehensible the mystery of a woman's beauty! For I am old, and I am her father, and yet I feel before her like a domestic servant in the presence of a ruler of the world. Surely she would drive a young man into madness and ecstasy. And did the Creator, forsooth! form this incarnation of the intoxication of woman to no purpose? Surely she is a husband's ideal correlative in human form! And then he said to her: My daughter, it is high time that you were married: for an unmarried daughter is a scandal in her father's house.

Then said Shrí: Dear father, do not speak thus. Let me live and die a maiden, for I do not wish to be married[40]. The King said: Daughter, what is this that you are saying? Is not a husband the very object of your birth? Shrí said: Do not even dream of a husband for me. And there is a reason for this: for I am different from other maidens. And hearing this, the King was perplexed. And he looked at Shrí under his brows, and said to himself: She speaks truth. Certainly this daughter of mine, if she be mine[41], is not like other maidens. For who ever saw her equal in beauty, or

---

[38] There is here an untranslateable play on the word *kamalahása*, which means both *the opening of a lotus bud*, and an *irresistible smile*.

[39] *wyatikara*, a word expressive of the *varying* lustre or *wavering* coruscation of jewels,

[40] cf. Callimachus: δός μοι παρθενίην αἰώνιον, ἄππα, φυλάσσειν.

[41] This touch arises from the beautiful word for a daughter, *átmajá*, i.e. *she that is born from yourself.*

who ever heard of a maiden objecting to be married[42]? Or was my minister right, and is she really some deity in disguise?

So day after day he continued to urge her and argue with her. But at last, finding that his efforts to move her were as vain as if he were trying to pierce a diamond with a cotton thread, he exclaimed in dismay: Surely my crimes in a former birth were numerous and appalling, seeing that their fruit is a daughter, whose obstinate and unintelligible prejudice against a husband runs counter to the nature of woman, and will be the means of destroying my salvation. Then at last Shrí said: Dear father, do not be angry, and I will tell you the truth. Know that I, too, wish for a husband, but only for one husband, and no other. Then said the King: And who, then, is that husband? Shrí said: I do not know. But he will come to claim me, from the Land of the Lotus of the Sun[43]. And where, said the King, is the Land of the Lotus of the Sun? Shrí said: I cannot tell. But in a dream I saw a lotus fall from heaven, and I heard a divine voice saying to me: Do not hurry, but wait: for there shall come to you a husband, from the Land of the Lotus of the Sun. For he was your husband in a former birth, and you shall know him by a sign. Then the King said: And what is the sign? Shrí said: I may not tell, for it is known only to the Deity and me. But now, either abandon my marriage, or if you can, find me a man who has seen the Land of the Lotus of the Sun, of caste becoming a king's daughter, and he shall be my husband. For him only will I marry, and none other.

---

[42] A case, perhaps, not absolutely unknown in the west: though beauty, like a fortress, must always like to be flattered by a siege. But in the land of the Hindus, marriage is like being born or dying, a matter of course, a thing necessary, inevitable, essential, *quod semper, quod ubique, quod ab omnibus.*

[43] There is, in the original here, a nuance not susceptible of direct translation. According to the Hindus, lotuses are divided into those of the Day and Night, whose lovers are the Sun and Moon. The Lotus in question is a Sun-lotus '*between the Twilights,*' i.e., buried in night, and deprived of the presence of the Sun. An allusion to the title of the story is thus introduced. But all this cannot be expressed in English, as it can in Sanskrit, by a single word.

And when the King heard this, he was astonished, and sat silent, looking at Shrí. And he said to himself: This is a strange story, and the conduct of this mysterious daughter of mine is inscrutable. What is this Land of the Lotus of the Sun? Is it a fancy, the capricious dream of a girl? Or does the dream really point to a previous existence? And he thought for a while, and then he said again: Perhaps it is better to do as she says, and endeavour to discover a man who has seen that Land. For where is the harm? For even if he is found, there will always be time to consider. And, moreover, in this way it may be that she will obtain a husband, whereas she will certainly not get married in any other. Better that she should get a husband, no matter how, no matter who, than remain a maiden to destroy us all.

Then he dismissed his daughter, and summoned his chamberlains, and said to them: Get criers, and send them through the city, and let them proclaim by beat of drum: That any high caste man, who has seen the Land of the Lotus of the Sun, shall share my kingdom, and marry my daughter. And his chamberlains wondered at hearing the order. But they went immediately, and told the criers the order of the King.

II. By Beat of Drum

So the criers went through the streets of the capital, beating drums and crying aloud: *Whatsoever high-caste man has been to the Land of the Lotus of the Sun, let him come to the King: he shall share the King's kingdom, and marry the King's daughter.* And hearing the proclamation, all the citizens and strangers in the city marvelled as they listened. For the fame of the beauty of the King's daughter had gone out into the three worlds. And buzzing like bees, they thronged around the criers, and ran up and down, everybody asking everybody else: What is this Land of the Lotus of the Sun? Where is it, or who has seen it? And a great uproar arose in the streets of the city, and they were full of noise and shouting: and the news was carried into the neighbouring kingdoms, and immediately crowds of people poured into Indirálaya from every part of Málwá and the Deckan and the North, and every quarter of the world, and together with the merchants and the working castes, who all abandoned their ordinary business, gathered in knots and stood about, asking eagerly for news of that Lotus Land, and its nature, and its locality, and its peculiarities. But no one could be found who had ever even heard of it, much less seen it. So day by day the proclamation sounded in the streets: and all day long the city was full of the din of shouting criers and beaten drums, and all night long sleep fled from the eyes of the citizens, as if in disgust at the noise that they made by day. But all was in vain: for not a man could they find, nor did anyone come forward to say: I have seen that Lotus Country: give me the reward.

And at last the citizens became enraged, alike with the King, and his daughter, and the Land of the Lotus, and themselves. And seeing this, the old King fell sick with anxiety: and he said to himself: My pretty daughter is as cunning as she is beautiful, and beyond a doubt this is some trick devised by her, to appease me, and avoid her bugbear of a husband, and befool us all. And now I fear that in their fury my subjects may break out into revolt, and refuse to pay taxes, or depose me. Out on my daughter and her blue eyes, and the cunning of women and their crooked hearts! Is there any such land in the world, as this Land of the Lotus of the Sun, of which in all my dominions, haunted by merchants and strangers from every quarter of the earth, no one has ever even so much as heard?

III. An Eclipse of the Sun

Now Kamalamitra, when he was separated from Anushayiní by the curse of the ascetic, fell down to earth, and was born as the son of a King of the Solar Race in a distant country. And his father gave him the name of Umra-Singh[44], for the astrologers said: He will live on earth like a lion, and run over it like his rival in the sky. And when he grew up, there was no one in that country who could match him in riding, or wrestling, or swordsmanship, or any other martial exercise: so that the people said of him: He looks like the very soul of the nature of a Kshatriya that has assumed a body suited to its deeds. Surely he is an incarnation of Kumára[45], come down to earth for the destruction of the King's enemies. And the women flocked around him like flies about honey, for their hearts were trampled to pieces, like lotuses, by the wild-elephant of his glorious youth, and their souls were intoxicated with the nectar of the beauty of his figure, and followed him about like captives chained in rows. But Umra-Singh laughed at them all, and even outdid the moon-

---

[44] The name is *Amarasinha*. But this is so certain to be a stumbling-block in an English mouth, that I have spelt it as it would be pronounced by a Hindu. (*Um* as in *drum*.) It means '*lion-god*' or '*god-lion*,' a name suited to a king of the line of the Sun.
[45] The War-god.

crested god [46], in that he drank continually the deadly poison of the ocean of their seductions, without even staining his throat.

Then one day his father said to him: Come, now, I have arranged your marriage with the daughter of my most powerful enemy: so shall we become friends by the method of conciliation. Umra-Singh said: Find another bridegroom, for I have married my sharp sword. So his father was annoyed, and said: What is this folly, and whence can I procure another bridegroom? But Umra-Singh was silent. And three times his father repeated his words. Then after a while, Umra-Singh said: Bridegroom or no bridegroom, I will not marry anybody but the lady of my dream. Then said his father: Who, then, is this lady of your dream? Umra-Singh said: I do not know. But every other month, on the last day of the dark fortnight, there comes to me in a dream a vision of a woman, floating on a pool of white lotuses, in a boat of sandal with silver oars. But who she is I cannot tell, and her face I can never see, for it is always turned away.

Then his father began to laugh, and deride him. But Umra-Singh cared no more for the stream of his derision than Maheshwara for the Ganges when it fell on his head. Then his father said: Dismiss this delusion, and prepare for the wedding: for I have arranged the ceremonies, and appointed the day. But Umra-Singh laughed, and said: Marry her thyself: for I tell thee, I will not marry anybody, but the lady of my dream. Then his father flew into a rage, and summoned his guards, and threw the prince[47] into prison, saying to himself: He shall stay there, with his dream to keep him company, till he learns to obey. But Umra-Singh persuaded his gaolers to let him escape, for the subjects loved him more than his father. And he fled away by night into another country, abandoning his royal position for the sake of his dream.

---

[46] Because, though Shiwa drank the *kálakuta* or deadly sea-poison, with impunity, still it left its mark on his throat, and dyed it blue.

[47] A *rajpoot* means only the son of a king, and it is to be observed that there were *rajpoots* in India long before the present 'Rajpoots' ever came there.

And then he went from city to city, and from one country to another, eluding the pursuit of the agents sent after him by his father to bring him back, till at last he came to Indirálayá. And he dived into a disreputable quarter of that city, like a frog into a well, and remained there disgusted with life and his relations, plunging into dissipation to drown his grief, and surrounded by gamblers and outcasts, counting the whole world as a straw, supporting himself on his own courage, and his dream. And little by little all he had melted away like snow in the sun of his generosity, or was swallowed up by the ocean of greedy gamblers, among whom he scattered it with an open hand, asking, like his ancestor [48], nothing in return. And at last, being reduced to extremity, clad in garments worn and ragged, which like clouds vainly obscuring the Lord of the Day, could not hide, but rather increased, the beauty of his form, with nothing left to eat or drink, he determined to abandon the body. So taking down his sword from the wall, and holding it in his hand, he went out of his wretched lodging, saying to himself: Death is better than dishonour and insignificance, hunger and the loathing of life: for what is death but the beginning of another life, which cannot be worse than this one, be it what it may? And who knows but that I may meet her in the next life whom I dream of in this? For she who is but a dream now, may be a reality in another birth, and I may discover that lotus pool, waiting for me in another life. Therefore now I will go outside the city wall, and find some deserted garden, and there I will cut off my own head, and offer it up to Durgá as a sacrifice.

And as he stood at the door of the house, pondering which way he should go, there fell on his ear, for the hundredth time, the sound of the beating of drums. And he listened, and heard the criers crying: *Whatsoever high-caste man has been to the Land of the Lotus of the Sun, let him come to the King: lie shall share the King's kingdom, and marry the King's daughter.* And Umra-Singh

---

[48] i.e. the Sun. There are double meanings in this period, comparing him to the Sun.

laughed, and said to himself: What! are they still looking for a man, who has seen the Land of the Lotus of the Sun? And how, then, did they know that there was such a land to be seen?

And then on a sudden he started, as if he had been bitten by a snake. And he struck his hand on his sword, and exclaimed: Ha! But if nobody has ever seen that land, and no one knows anything about it, then, if one should come and say: Lo: I have seen it: who could discern whether he was speaking the truth or telling a lie? For who can compare the description with a reality which neither he nor anyone else ever saw? So what is to hinder me from going to the King and saying: I have seen that Lotus Land, and now, give me the reward? For here I am, about to put myself to death; and what greater evil can befall me at the hands of the King, even though he should discover the deceit? And yet, how can he? For who knows what that land is like, or even where it is? But if, on the contrary, I get credit, then I shall obtain, not only this far-famed daughter, for whom I care nothing, but also the resources of his kingdom; and with them I can equip an army, and go and compel my father to restore me to my position. So where is the harm? or rather, is it not pure gain, and no loss, to make the attempt and abide the result, whether I live or die?

Then instantly, without hesitation, he went up to the criers, and said to them: Cease your crying, and take me to the King, for I have seen that Lotus Land. But the criers, when they heard what he said, could not believe their ears, and almost abandoned the body from excess of joy. For they were almost dead from exhaustion, and continual shouting all day long. And they danced like peacocks at the sight of the first cloud in the rainy season, and caught him in their arms, holding him as if they were afraid he would escape, to carry him away, like a precious jewel, to the King. And the news ran through the city like fire in a dry wood: There has been found a man who has seen the Land of the Lotus of the Sun. And a vast crowd of people ran from every street, and pressed around him, and accompanied him to the palace, and stood before it, tossing like the sea, while the guards took him in to the King.

But when the King heard the news, he wept for joy. And Umra-Singh seemed in his eyes like a draught of nectar, and like the fulfilment of all his desires in bodily form. And he said to him: O thou unspeakably delightful son-in-law that shall be, hast thou really set eyes on that accursed Land of the Lotus of the Sun? And Umra-Singh said boldly: yes, I have seen it, and I know it well. Then immediately the King in his impatience ran himself to his daughter's apartments, and exclaimed: The bridegroom is found, by the favour of the Lord of Obstacles. Here is a Rajpoot who has seen the Land of the Lotus of the Sun. So prepare for the marriage without delay.

Then said Shrí: Dear father, there is no hurry in this matter. And how do you know that this man is speaking the truth, or is not, rather, some impostor, who only wishes to secure me and half your kingdom, by falsely asserting that he has seen, what in fact he never has seen. For the world is full of such crafty rogues, who go about, like cranes, fishing in the wealth of Kings, like pools. Bring him therefore first to me, to examine him; and thereafter we shall see, whether it is time to prepare the marriage ceremonies, or not.

So the King said: Be it so. And he sent for Umra-Singh, and brought him into the presence of Shrí.

And Shrí looked and saw him standing, sword in hand, tall, and lean in the waist like a hungry lion, with shoulders like those of a bull, and long arms, and all the royal marks of a King. And she would have despised him, for his rags and his nakedness, and yet for all that she would, she could not, but felt herself drawn towards him against her will. For her heart was stirred within her at the sight of him, and dim suggestions of that former birth, which she had forgotten, struggled in her soul, and strove to rise up out of its depths. And she stood, gazing at him in silence, with eyes that looked at him but did not see him, like those of one that listens to the tones of a long-forgotten voice, sounding in the hall of memory, and awakening longing and fond regret. And as she gazed, she poured over him a flood of blue colour out of her wondrous doubtful eyes.

And Umra-Singh looked at her, and the whole world vanished from his sight in a mass of blue. And he reeled under the blow of her glances, which struck him mercilessly like a club, and time and space fled from his soul, which was filled with colour, and tears, and laughter and pain, and he gasped for breath. For the sight of her half-remembered eyes clutched his heart, and stopped its beating like an iron band. And in that moment there rose before him the dream-woman of the lotus pool, and he knew that it was Shrí.

So they two stood there, like pictures painted on a wall, gazing at each other, and groping in vain for recollection in the darkness of oblivion[49], like shadows in a dream. And then, after a while, Shrí came to herself. And she said slowly: So thou hast seen the Land of the Lotus of the Sun? Then mention its peculiarities, and tell me how thou didst arrive at it.

But Umra-Singh stammered and hesitated. For her eyes had deprived him of his reason, and he could think of nothing else. And all his audacity had vanished, and become timidity, and he faltered, and spoke, not knowing what he said, with a voice that refused its office, and sounded in his ears like that of another man. And he said: Lady, I went I know not how, and wandered I know not how long, among wastes and deserts and mountains I know

---

[49] *adrishta*: a peculiar technical term, meaning something that has its roots in the *unseen* circumstances of a former birth.

not how high, till I came to a land I know not where, called the Land of the Lotus of the Sun, I know not why[50].

But as he spoke, the spell was broken, and Shrí woke as it were from a dream. And she saw before her only a ragged Rajpoot, stumbling in his tale, and abashed before her, and unable to support his knavery even by a clever lie. And she was ashamed, and angry with herself, and as she listened, she was suddenly seized with a fit of laughter. And she exclaimed: Hark! hark! to this high-caste hero; listen to his lay of a Lotus Land! He went he knew not where, and did he knew not what, and began at the beginning, and ended at the end. So she laughed and mocked him, while he stood before her as it were in a swoon, hearing only the music of her voice, and quailing like a coward before the fire in her scornful eyes.

Then suddenly Shrí clapped her hands in his face, and exclaimed: Dost thou hear, or art thou deaf as well as dumb? Art thou a Rajpoot, and yet could'st thou not find courage enough to carry out thy imposition to the end? Strange! that such a body could be chosen by the Creator as the receptacle of such a soul. And she turned to the King, and said: Dear Father, it is as I said, and as you see, this fellow is but a rogue. Put him out, therefore; and yet, do him no harm. For though he is a knave, yet he is a handsome knave, and deserves rather contempt and laughter, than punishment and blows.

Then the King said to his guards: Take this impostor, and thrust him out into the street. So the guards seized Umra-Singh, who offered no resistance, and threw him out into the street, raining upon him as he went a shower of kicks and blows. And immediately the criers went round the city as before, beating drums and crying aloud: *Whatsoever high-caste man has been to*

---

[50] No translator can give the alliterative jingle of the *rathás* and *tathás*, *vads* and *tads* of this and the answer of Shrí below.

40

the Land of the Lotus of the Sun, let him come to the King: he shall share the King's kingdom, and marry the King's daughter.

IV. Inspiration

But Umra-Singh lay in the street, more like a dead than a living man, covered with bruises and bereft of sense. And the people crowded round him, jeering and scouting and pointing at him, and giving him blows and kicks. And he looked in the midst of those base mockers like a black antelope smitten by the hunters with a mortal wound, and surrounded by a troop of chattering monkeys. Then by and by those scoffers left him lying, and went every man his way, for the sun was going down. And after a while, he came to himself, and rose up, though with difficulty, from the ground, and wandered away with stumbling feet, till he came to a tank in a deserted quarter, and lay down on its brink to rest. And sore though he was in all his limbs, he never felt the pain of his body: but his eyes were dazed with the blue glory of the bitter scorn of the eyes of Shrí, and the sound of her voice and her laughter rang in his ears, and in his heart was shame. So he lay long, gazing at the image of Shrí as it floated before him, and stung his soul like the teeth of a serpent, and yet soothed it like sandal, while the moon rose in the sky. And then suddenly he sat up, and looked round. And he saw the tank, and the trees, and the moon's image in the water, and remembered where he was, and all that had occurred. And he sighed deeply, and said to himself: Woe is me! I have, like a dishonest gambler, cast my die, and lost the game. And now, I have gained no kingdom and no King's daughter, but only blows and shame. Alas! no sooner had I found my dream than again I lost her, through the terrible operation of sins committed in a former birth. So now, nothing remains but to do as quickly as possible what I was about to do before I went to the palace, and put myself, in very truth, to death. For life seemed unendurable, before I had found the woman of my dream: but now it is worse by far, since I have found her only to become in her eyes a thing of scorn, more horrible than a hundred deaths.

And he took his sword, and felt the sharpness of its edge, and put it to his throat. And as it touched his skin, at that moment he heard in the silence of the night the voice of a warder, singing as he went his round upon the city wall: *Whatsoever high-caste man has been to the Land of the Lotus of the Sun, let him come to the ling: he shall share the King's kingdom and marry the King's daughter.* And the sword fell from his hand, and he sprang to his feet, and exclaimed: What! she is for the man who has seen the Land of the Lotus, and here am I, a Rajpoot of the Race of the Sun, dreaming of death by this moonlit tank, while the Land of the Lotus is yet unfound! Now will I find that Lotus Country, be it where it may, and then come back and claim her, not as I did before, in jest, but by the right of the seer and the seen.

And instantly he picked up his sword, and threw it into the air. And the sword turned like a wheel, flashing in the moonlight, and fell back to the ground. Then Umra-Singh took it up, and immediately went out of the city, making for the quarter pointed out like a finger by the blade of his sword.

V. Nightwalker

And then as a black bee roves from flower to flower he wandered from city to city, and from one country to another: and he went north and east and west and south, till the elephants of the eight quarters knew him as it were by sight. Yet he never found anyone who could tell him his way, or had ever heard the name of the Land of the Lotus of the Sun. And meanwhile the suns of the hot seasons burned him like a furnace, and the cold seasons froze the blood in his veins, and the rains roared over his head like a wild-elephant, and at the last, he said to himself: Now for thrice six seasons have I been seeking, and yet I know no more of my way to the Land of the Lotus than I did before. And undoubtedly, if such a Land exists in the world, it can be known only to the birds of the air. Therefore now I will abandon the dwellings of men, and enter the Great Forest, for only in this way will it ever be possible for me to discover a land of which no human being has ever heard.

So he went into the forest and proceeded onward, turning his face to the south. Then as he went the trees grew thicker and thicker, and taller and taller, till they shut out the light of the sun. And at last there came a day when he looked before him, and saw only a darkness like that of the mouth of death: and he looked behind him, and saw the light of evening glimmering a great way off, as if afraid to keep him company. And as he went on slowly, feeling his way with the point of his sword, suddenly in the darkness another face peered into his own, and stuck out at him a long red tongue. And Umra-Singh started back, and looked, and saw before him a root-eating Wairágí [51] clad in a coat of bark, with long hair, and nails like the claws of a bird, and his legs and arms were bare, and his skin like that on the foot of an elephant:

Then said Umra-Singh: Father, what art thou doing here, and why dost thou stick out at me thy tongue? The Wairágí said: Son, what art thou doing here, in a wood full of nothing but trees and Rákshasas[52], and dark as the Hair of the Great God, of which it is an earthly copy? Umra-Singh said: I am a Rajpoot who has quarrelled with his relations, and I am looking for the Land of the Lotus of the Sun. Then said the Wairágí: They are very few that wish to find that Lotus Land; and fewer still who find it; fewest of all those, that having found it ever return. Then Umra-Singh said, in astonishment: And dost thou know that Lotus Land? Tell me how I must go to reach it. Then the Wairágí laughed, and said: Ha! ha! Thou art one more ready to ask than to answer questions: but I give nothing for nothing. Know, that I also have all my life been looking, not for one way only, but for three. And now, if thou wilt tell me my three ways, I will tell thee thine.

Then said Umra-Singh: One for three is no bargain; but what, then, are thy lost ways? The Wairágí said: All my life I have tried to discover the Way of the World, and the Way of Woman, and the Way of Emancipation[53], and yet could never hit on the truth as to any one of them. And this is a wonderful thing. For anything characteristic of multitudes must be very common: and yet how can that which is common escape the notice of all? Tell

---

[51] This term denotes one who has turned his back on the world, and become free from passion. Its meaning can best be learned from the third section of the Centuries of Bhartrihari, devoted to it. (*wair-* rhymes with *fire*.)

[52] *Jinn*, ogres, vampires, goblins, &c., are all but differentiations of the Hindu *Rákskasa*, which is what the geologist calls a 'synthetic type' of evil being, whose special feature is its power of changing its shape at will (*Kámarupa*).

[53] There is here an untranslateable play on the word *tripathagá, the three-way-goer*, i.e. the Ganges, which flows in three *Ways*--in heaven, earth, and hell. The hermit asks, as we might say, for *the source of the Nile*.

45

me, then, the Way of the World, and I will tell thee in return a third of thy way to the Land of the Lotus of the Sun.

Then said Umra-Singh: Thou puttest a knotty question, and drivest a hard bargain; nevertheless, I will give thee an answer, for the sake of my own way and the blue eyes of Shrí. Know, that this is the Way of the World. There was formerly, on the banks of Ganges, an old empty temple of Shiwa. And one night, in the rainy season, an old female ascetic entered the temple, to shelter herself from the storm. And just after her there came in an owl for the same purpose. Now in the roof of that temple there lived a number of the caste[54] of bats, that never left the temple precincts. And seeing the owl, they said to the old woman: Who art thou, and what kind of animal is this? Then the old woman said: I am the Goddess Saraswatí, and this is the peacock on which I ride[55]. Then, the storm being over, that old impostor went away. But the owl, being pleased with the temple as a place of residence, remained; and the bats paid it divine honours. Then some years afterwards, it happened, that a real peacock entered the temple. And the bats said to it: What kind of animal art thou? The peacock said: I am a peacock. The bats replied: Out on thee, thou impostor! what is this folly? The peacock said: I am a peacock, the son of a peacock, and the carriage of the Goddess Saraswatí is a hereditary office in our caste. The bats said: Thou art a liar, and the son of a liar; dost thou know better than the Goddess herself? And they drove the peacock out of the temple, and paid, as formerly, worship to the owl.

Then said the Wairágí: Rajpoot, thou hast opened my eyes. Learn now from me a portion of thy own way. And he lay down on the ground, and suddenly abandoning the form of a hermit, became a weasel, which stuck out at Umra-Singh a long red tongue, and entered the ground by a hole, and disappeared. And as Umra-Singh stooped down to examine the hole, he saw the Wairágí

---

[54] The proper word for caste is *játi, gens.*
[55] Every Hindu god or goddess has his or her peculiar animal vehicle (*wáhana*).

46

again beside him in his old shape, save that he continued to stick out of his mouth the weasel's tongue, And he said, angrily: What is this delusion of a weasel, and why dost thou stick out thy tongue? Then said the Wairágí: Ho! ho! I have shown thee a way for a way, and one riddle for another. And now, tell me the Way of a Woman, and learn yet another third of thy own road.

Then Umra-Singh said to himself: Surely this is no hermit, but a vile Rákshasa, who only seeks to delude me. Nevertheless, I will give him an answer, for the sake of my way, and the blue light in the eyes of Shrí. And he said to the Wairágí: Know, then, that the Way of a Woman is this: There dwelt long ago, in the Windhya forest, an old Rishi. And the gods, being jealous of his austerities, sent to interrupt his devotions a heavenly nymph. Then that old Rishi, overcome by her beauty, yielded to the temptation, and had by her a daughter. But afterwards, repenting of his fall, he burned out his eyes with a fiery cane, saying: Perish, ye causes of perishable illusions: and so became blind. Then his daughter grew up alone with that old blind sage in the forest. And she was more beautiful than any woman in the three worlds. Verily, had the God of Love seen .her, he would instantly have abandoned Rati and Príti [56], counting them but as her domestic servants. And she dressed in bark garments, with no mirror but the pools of the forest. Then one day a crow that was acquainted with cities came to her and said: Why dost thou live here, with no companion but an old blind father, who cannot even see thee, and does not know the value of his pearl? The whole world does not contain a beauty equal to thine. Go and show thyself in cities, and I tell thee, the Kings of the earth would quit their kingdoms, and follow thee about like a swarm of bees. Then said the Rishí's daughter: And who, then, would fetch for my father his sacrificial fuel, or water to cook his cakes of rice and milk? And she drove away the crow, and lived on in the forest, serving her father, and at the last became old, and died in the forest, and no man ever saw her face.

---

[56] Pleasure and Joy, the two wives of the God of Love.

Then said the Wairági: Thou foolish Rajpoot, I asked thee for the Way of a Woman, and thou hast told me the Way of Emancipation. Then said Umra-Singh: Thou miserable root-eater, since the creation every woman has sacrificed herself for another, or else she was not a woman, for this is the nature of them all. Then said the Wairági: Learn now from me, another portion of thy own way. And as Umra-Singh watched him, suddenly that deceitful Wairági became a bat, and stuck out at him again his tongue, and flew away through the trees. And Umra-Singh said to himself: Beyond a doubt this is no ascetic, but the very King of Rákshasas; nevertheless, he shall tell me my road, if he comes again, or it shall be the worse for him. And suddenly again he saw the Wairági standing by his side, and sticking out at him, as before, his tongue. And he said to Umra-Singh: Now thou hast only to tell me the Way of Salvation, and thy own way will be clear before thee.

Then said Umra-Singh: Thou art but an old Rákshasa; nevertheless, once more will I give thee an answer, for the sake of my way, and the colour of the eyes of Shrí. Know, that the Way of Emancipation is this: There was formerly a King of the race of the Sun, and he was very old, and all his hair was as white as the uppermost peak of the Snowy mountain. And one day he looked from his palace window, and saw in the street a child, drawing behind it a toycart. And the cart fell, and was broken, and the child cried over its broken toy. Now it happened, by the ordinance of fate, that long ago, when he was himself a child, exactly the same thing had happened to that old King. And as he looked at the child, suddenly the years were annihilated, and became as nothing. And like a picture he saw before him, the image of himself, a child. And seized with grief, and an unutterable longing for the repetition of his life, he exclaimed: O Maheshwara, Maheshwara, let me live my life again. Then suddenly Maheshwara stood before him, and laughed, and said: Remember thy former births. And suddenly memory came upon that old King, and out of the darkness of the past there rose before him the series of his former lives. And Maheshwara said: See, nine and ninety times, in nine and ninety births, thou hast made of me the same request, and now this is a hundred. And every time I have given thee thy wish, in vain. For every time thou hast forgotten, and hast known the value of thy youth only after becoming old. Then said the old King: How, then, can emancipation be obtained? Maheshwara said: It depends not on time, but knowledge: and even an instant can bring it when ten thousand years have failed. And thou hast but a little left of life, yet even to thee knowledge may come before the end. Then he disappeared. Now that old King had a daughter whom he loved better than his own soul. And, even while he spoke with Maheshwara, she was bitten by a snake and died, and he did not know it, for they feared to tell him. So he went as usual to see his daughter. And when he entered her room, he looked, and saw her lying still. And as he watched her, there came a fly, which buzzed about her, and settled on her lips. Then horror came on that old King, and illusion fell suddenly from his eyes, and the desire of life was destroyed in him at its root. And he turned, and went without waiting to the Ganges, and remained there a few years washing away his crimes, like one to whom life and death are the same, and at last entered the river, and it drowned him, and carried his body out to sea.

Then said the Wairágí: Now shalt thou have emancipation from thy own ignorance, as to thy way to the Land of the Lotus of the Sun. And he stuck out at Umra-Singh his tongue. But Umra-Singh suddenly struck at him a blow of his sword, and as luck would have it, he cut off the end of his tongue. And he said to him: Beware lest I kill thee, thou old impostor. I will waste no more time expecting to hear from thee my way to the Land of the Lotus, but find it in spite of thee. Then the Wairágí suddenly assumed a terrific form, and exclaimed: Woe to thee, thou unlucky Rajpoot. For thou art now in the land, not of lotuses, but of Rákshasas, of whom I am the chief. And my subjects shall beset thee with illusions, like the sins of thy former birth in visible form; and there wait for thee the Night-walkers, Ulupí, and the Cow-killer, and the Hairy Grabber, and the Icy Chiller, and the Flap-eared Buzzer, and the awful Watcher in his pits of sand, and others without number[57]: and even shouldst thou escape them all, and reach the Lotus Land, thou hast

---

[57] These names, which recall certain passages in the Rámayan, lose much of their effect in translation. *goghna,* 'cow-killer,' has a curious history. Because of old a cow could be killed *only* for a guest of great honour, a word of the most horrible signification actually acquired one honourable meaning, i.e. a guest of a high order.

still to return. And he vanished with a shout of laughter, and Umra-Singh was left alone.

VI. A Lotus of the Night

Then he said to himself: Though I cut off the tongue of this ill-omened Wairágí, yet he never told me my way. And he went on, sword in hand, along a silver path, among trees that resembled Rákshasas, for they let in through the hair of their branches the light of the moon, which peered down at him as if out of curiosity, and lit him on his way as if in admiration of his courage. And as he went, gradually the trees grew rarer, and at length he looked before him, and saw in a clear space a dark blue forest pool, studded with moon-lotuses, as if created to mock the expanse of heaven bespangled with its stars, a mirror formed by Wedasa [58] to reproduce another world below. And all about it flitted fireflies, looking like swarms of bees that had returned with torches, unable to endure separation at night from the lotus flowers which they loved all day.

And as he gazed into the water, he saw in its smooth mirror the image of a woman, dancing. And as she danced, her robes of the colour of grass fluttered in the wind produced by her own movement over the curves of her limbs; and drops of water sparkled in the moonlight like gems on her bosom, which rose and fell like a wave of the sea in and out of the shadow of her hair: for that hair resembled a mass of the essence of the blackness of night. And she chanted as she danced with a voice that sounded like a spell, and fanned the ear like a breeze from the Malaya

---

[58] The Creator.

mountain [59]. Then Umra-Singh raised his eyes, and saw the original of that water-painted woman-image, dancing on the other side of the pool.

Then she looked across and saw him, and their eyes met, travelling over the pool. And instantly she stopped her singing and dancing, and clapped her hands, and called to him like a *Kokila*: Come over to me, thou handsome stranger, for I am weary of dancing alone, and I have a question to ask thee. And she leaned against a tree and stood waiting, with one hand on the trunk of the tree and the other on her hip, and a heaving breast: and she looked like a feminine incarnation of the essence of the agitation of the ocean, stirred by the sight of the moon. And Umra-Singh looked at her, and said to himself: Certainly the daughters of Rákshasas are more dangerous than their fathers. And now it is well, that I am fenced by the blue eyes of Shrí like a suit of armour, otherwise the glances of this forest maiden would like an axe long ago have cleft my heart in two.

Then he went round the edge of the pool, and found her on the other side. And she beckoned to him as he drew near with a bangled hand, and moving lips, and eyes that shone in the moonlight like the eyes of a snake. And she came and stood before him, and put her hand on his shoulder with a touch like a leaf, and looked up into his face with a smile, and said: I am Ulupí, a Daitya's [60] daughter, and here I live in the forest alone, with none to whom to compare myself, save my own image in the water. Tell me, for thou hast seen other women, hast thou ever met with eyes more beautiful than mine? And Umra-Singh looked down into them as into two dark pools, and he felt them pounding his heart like a pair of fists [61]. And he said to himself: She may well ask, and now, but for one other pair, her eyes need

---

[59] From which the sandal wood comes.
[60] A kind of demon, 'a son of Diti.' (Pronounce *dait-* as *white.*)
[61] A reminiscence of Bhartrihari.

52

fear no rivals. But he said to her: Beauty[62], thine eyes are well enough: nevertheless the ocean has many gems, and doubtless each thinks itself the best: but the Koustubha [63] is above them all.

Then a cloud came over her face, and she flung away from him in disdain, and stood pouting like a child. And suddenly she turned again, and put up to her head the graceful creepers of her round arms, and undid the knot of her hair, and shook it. And it fell, like midnight, about those stars her eyes, and wrapped her all over like a veil, and rolled down round her feet and along the ground, like a black serpent. Then with her hand she put it away from her face, and shot through its meshes a subtle smile, and said: At least thou hast never seen the equal of my hair? And Umra-Singh felt her glance strike him like a thunderbolt out of a cloud. And he said to himself: Well may she ask; and now, if my soul were not already snared in the long lashes of the eyes of Slid, it would be netted like a quail in this extraordinary mass of never-ending hair. But he said: Beauty, lovely at night is the heaven with its stars, but lovelier still the dark blue sea, in which they are reflected, for it contains all their beauty, and adds another of its own.

Then Ulupí was very angry, and she stood with flashing eyes, swelling with rage. And suddenly she stooped, and gathered up her hair in her arm, and came up to Umra-Singh, and flung it round him like a noose, and whispered in his ear, with lips that caressed it as they moved: O foolish bee[64], I am but a lotus of the night: yet why despise me, in comparison with the absent lotus of the day? It is hot and dusty, and I am cool and fragrant as the nectar of that moon in whose light I blow. And Umra-Singh trembled. For there came from her hair a strange wind, like a cloud of the sweet of a thousand scents, that lured his soul to

---

[62] Nothing can translate *bálá*. It means child, woman, beauty, *beauté-de-diable*.
[63] Wishnu's great breast-jewel (*Kou* as *cow*).

[64] This word here used may mean either a *bee* or a *lover* or a *wanderer* (*bhramara*).

listen and dream in the lulling murmur of her mouth. And as he closed his eyes for fear, he saw before him the blue scorn in the eyes of Shrí, and the sound of her laughter and the noise of the drums and the voices of the criers boomed in his ear, and drowned Ulupí's spell. And he shook himself free from her hair, and said: Beauty, I am a Rajpoot of the race of the Sun: what have I to do with a lotus of the moon?

Then Ulupí screamed, like a wounded elephant. And she seized him by the arm and shook him violently, and exclaimed: Hast thou a stone within thy breast, instead of a heart, that my beauty cannot touch thee? For I know that I am beautiful, and there is not beauty like mine in the three worlds. And Umra-Singh looked at her, and wondered, for her fury made her more lovely than before. And he said: O daughter of a Daitya, thou speakest the truth: yet a vessel that is full can hold no more, be the liquor what it may, and such is my heart. Let me now pass by thee, as undeserving thy regard: for I am bound for the Land of the Lotus of the Sun. Then said Ulupí, with a stamp of her foot: Fool! thou shalt never see that Lotus Land.

And she looked at him with a jeering laugh: and instantly she sat down, and wound herself up in her long hair, and began to weep. And as she wept, the tears ran down from her eyes like a river, and fell into the lake. Immediately the lake began to rise and swell, and flood the wood with water. And as Umra-Singh stood gazing at her with astonishment, he found himself standing in a vast marsh, with the trees of the forest for rushes. And he looked, and lo! suddenly that delusive daughter of a Daitya became a mist, and floated away over the water like vapour. And Umra-Singh heard her laughter dying away in the distance as she went, and he was left alone in the wood, with the water up to his waist.

VII. The Silver Swans

And as the water kept on rising, rising, Umra-Singh said to himself: Extraordinary is the guile of women, and copious their tears, but this daughter of a Daitya surely surpasses them all. For who ever heard of tears that, like rivers, could flood a quarter of the world? But in the meanwhile, before I find my death in these rising waters, it is better to take refuge in a tree. So he climbed up into a tree, and looked out over the water, on which the mist hung in the moonlight like a curtain of silver on a floor of lapis-lazuli. And he said to himself: Is this merely an illusion, or rather, is not this wood well named, being in very truth the matted hair of the great god, with these trees for hairs, and this water for the Ganges that wanders among them[65], and yonder moon the very ornament of the moon-crested god? But this water goes on rising, and I must ascend higher into the tree.

So he climbed up, and up, and as he climbed, the water rose after him, higher and higher, until at last he could see nothing but the water, and the moon, and the tree that stretched away above him into the sky. And as he went, he said to himself: Up I must go, for there is no other resource: and now, unless like the husband of

---

[65] The Ganges fell from heaven, and Shiwa caught it on his head, where it wandered in his hair for a thousand years before it could find its way down. A legend which doubtless has reference to the vast plateaux of the Himálaya and Tibet.

Shrí[66]. I could save myself on the back of a tortoise from this very sea of water, I must surely be destroyed. For unless this extraordinary tree has no top, I must presently reach it, and meet with my death at the same time. And even without the water, as to how I am to get down again, I have not an idea. So he continued to climb and climb, while the water rose, and the moon sank, and the night gradually came to an end.

And then the sun rose over the eastern mountain, and began like himself to climb up into the sky. And the sweat poured from his limbs, and at last he stopped, overcome with fatigue. And he said to himself: Now I can go no further. Since I must now in any case perish, why should I go on climbing in vain? For surely I am on the very roof of the world, and alone with the sun in the sky.

And as he looked down, suddenly he saw before him no water and no tree, and his head grew dizzy, and his vision swam, and he could scarcely believe his eyes.

For he stood on the peak of a high mountain, in the very zenith of the sky. And all round him, and all before him, and behind him, was a vast desert of burning sand, that stretched away to the very limit of the range of sight, and on its edges rested the quarters of heaven. And it glowed in the fire of the sun's rays like a furnace, and was furrowed and pitted with holes and chasms; and its surface rose and fell, as he watched it, like a woman's breast, and it looked as if it were alive, though it was in truth the home of death. And as he gazed, he saw, how over it there crawled swiftly living things with pointed tails, of the colour of sand, which entered the desert by the holes, and issued from them, and at length stood still, and became invisible, save that their tails never rested, and their bright eyes stood out of the sand to watch. And it seemed to Umra-Singh, in the loneliness of that vast solitude, that all those hideous Eyes sought him out, and fastened

---

[66] He compares himself to the husband of the other Shrí, i.e. the Goddess of Beauty, or Wishnu, whose second incarnation was that of a tortoise.

on him, and rested on him alone, saying to him as it were: Thou canst not escape.

And then he said to himself: Now there is indeed no help for me, and beyond a doubt, my end has come. For to remain here is impossible, and equally certain the death that lies, either in going forward or going back. And yet I could wish to die, if at all, not in the presence of eyes such as these, but in the colour of the eyes of Shrí. Yet how shall I escape the vigilance of yonder dreadful Dwellers in the Sand, wading with difficulty in its substance that will sink under my feet like the waves of the sea, but over which they scud like the shadow of a cloud?

So all day he remained on that high place, not daring to descend. And then at length the sun went to his rest in the western quarter, and the moon rose, and was reflected in the bright eyes of those sand-haunting Rákshasas, which glittered in the distance on the dark desert like drops of water on the leaf of a black lotus. And all night long Umra-Singh lay and watched them, as a bird watches the eyes of a snake.

Then in the early dawn he looked, and as the light of morning began to glimmer in the distance on the edge of the world, he saw far away in the pale air two dark specks in the sky. And as he gazed, they grew larger and rapidly approached him, sending back to him, like mirrors, the red rays of the rising sun. And they drew nearer, and he saw that they were a pair of silver Swans, carrying in their bills the dead body of a third, of gold. So these two Swans crossed over that dreadful desert with the rapidity of the lightning that resembled them, and settled beside him on the hill, to rest.

Then said Umra-Singh: Hail! ye fair birds: surely ye are no birds, but deities, fallen into these bodies of swans by reason of a curse. Whence come ye, and whither go ye, and what is this dead golden body that ye carry as ye go? Then said the Swans: We are carrying home the body of our king, far away to the Mánasa lake. For he died yesterday, in the Land of the Lotus of the Sun. And now we must bear him ever onward swiftly to his own country, that the funeral ceremonies may duly be performed.

But when Umra-Singh heard them name the Land of the Lotus, his heart leaped in his breast. And sword in hand, he rushed on the dead body with a shout. And he said to the Swans: As you carried him hither from that Land of the Lotus of the Sun, so swear now, that you will carry me first back thither, leaving him here till you return: otherwise I will keep him, and cut you to pieces.

Then seeing that there was no help for it, the Swans said: Be it so: and they bound themselves to him by an oath. And then Umra-Singh took hold of them by the neck, one in each hand; and they stretched out their necks, and flew away with him over the desert as he hung. And he left far behind him the eyes of those hideous Rákshasas glowing in the sand as if with rage to see him escape: and after a long while, they came to the edge of the desert. And Umra-Singh looked down and saw, far below him, the blue sea, shimmering like the eyes of Shrí. And at a distance in the water, like a dusky jewel on a purple carpet, he saw an island, with a city on it. So he said to the Swans: What is that which I see below me? And they said: It is the Land of the Lotus of the Sun.

Then in his delight, Umra-Singh let go his hold, and clapped his hands. And instantly he fell down like a stone into the sea. But the Swans returned swiftly over the desert to the body which they had left upon the hill.

VIII. The Land of the Lotus

But Umra-Singh rose out of the water like a fowl, and saw the Land of the Lotus away on the sea before him. And he shouted for joy, and began to swim in that direction. And he swam on all day, and at last, though with difficulty, he reached the shore, when his strength was almost gone. And he crept up out of the water, as the sun was going down; and overcome with weariness, he lay down, there where he came up out of the sea, and fell asleep. And all night long he slept, and all day; and when the moon had risen again, full and round, as if to see whether he was still there, he awoke.

And then he stood up, and rubbed his eyes, and exclaimed: Ha! now I am at my journey's end, and all its dangers are gone like dreams. And this is that wonderful Land of the Lotus of the Sun, of which no one in Indirálayá had ever heard! So now that I am here, what remains for me to do, but to leave it, and go back again as quickly as possible. For I desired to find it, only to say that I had been there. And yet when I return, who will believe me? It were better, now that I am here, to examine it, and learn its peculiarities, that I may not twice meet with the treatment due to impostors.

So he went up from the shore, and through the streets of the city, that lay before him, black and white, in the rays of the silver moon. And he met nobody, but it was empty, and dark as a barren womb, and silent as a stone incarnation of the spirit of

59

death. And as he wandered up and down, he came at last to a great palace, whose doors stood wide open, as much as to say: Come in. So he went in, and passed along, wondering, with echoing steps, from room to room. Then on a sudden he entered a door, and found himself in a vast hall, whose walls were pierced with tall windows, through which the moonlight fell, cold as camphor, on moon-stones that hung in clusters from the roof. And from them the nectar fell slowly, drop by drop, upon the floor. And at the far end of the room, on a golden couch, he saw lying a dead body, covered with a white pall.

Then he said to himself: What is this wonder, and who can it be that lies here, alone in this empty hall? And he moved on slowly, through the lights of the windows and the shadows of the walls, till he came up to the end of the hall, and stood beside the couch. And he stooped down, and lifted up the edge of the pall, and uncovered the face, and looked, and lo! it was the face of Shrí.

And Umra-Singh was so astounded, that he leaped into the air, and uttered a cry: and he let his sword fall with a crash upon the crystal floor. And he said to himself: Is it a dream, or is it an illusion? Lo! I left her living in Indirálayá, and I have travelled over the three worlds, and here at the end of space I find her again, lying dead in this empty hall!

So he stood, like a picture on a wall, gazing in silence at the face of Shrí, while the night wore away, and the moon travelled on, and the nectar from the moonstones fell slowly, drop by drop, upon the ground, and the shadows moved round upon the floor. And at last, after a long while, he came to himself. And he let the pall fall from his hand, recovering the face. And he stooped down, and took up his sword, and went slowly out of that strange hall, and sat down on the steps of a marble tank, and fell into a waking dream. And as he gazed into vacancy, he saw before him the blue ocean of the eyes of Shrí; and his memory echoed with faint murmurs of the sound of drums and the voices of criers; and they

60

filled his soul with whispers coming from an infinite distance across the years of separation, until at length the sun rose.

Then Umra-Singh rose up also, and he struck his forehead with his hand. And he exclaimed: I cannot tell, whether it is reality, or whether it is a dream. But this I know, that now I must get back without delay to Indirálayá, and cross, somehow or other, over that sea, and that terrible desert, and through that hideous wood, and tell my story to the King, and claim my bride. But first I will bathe in yonder pool: for my heart is heavy, and my head aches, for all that I have endured during the night, and all that I have seen.

And he went down the steps, and plunged into the waters of the pool.

IX. Recognition

And as he rose from the water, there rang in his ears, loud and clear, the sound of the beating of drums. And he listened, and heard the criers crying: *Whatsoever high-caste man has been to the Land of the Lotus of the Sun, let him come to the King: he shall share the King's kingdom, and marry the King's daughter.* And he looked round. Lo! he was standing in that very tank in Indirálayá, from which he had started, years before, to find the Land of the Lotus of the Sun. Then in his amazement, his flesh crept, and his hair stood on end. And he stood in the pool like a pillar of stone, with the water streaming from his body, and doubt bewildering his soul. And he said to himself: Is it indeed reality, or is it a dream? And what has become of the Land of the Lotus, and all my toil? For here I am in Indirálayá, and there are the very criers whom I left behind me, crying, and beating, just as they did before, their drums!

And then suddenly he uttered a shout, and exclaimed: Well, now I will go to the King, for the time has come to claim the reward. And he leaped out of the water, and ran up the steps like one that is mad, and went up to the criers, and said to them: Cease this useless crying, and this empty beating of drums, and take me quickly to the King, for I have seen that Lotus Land. And the criers did not recognise him, but they were full of joy at hearing his words: for their crying had made them weary of life. So as they were preparing to take him to the King, he clapped his hands, and said again: Quick! delay not! but make haste, great haste! or else my heart will break. For I endured separation, when union seemed at a distance, with ease: but now that the moment of re-union approaches, my heart is breaking: every moment seems an age: and if you delay long, I cannot endure. Then the criers made great haste, and brought him as quickly as possible to the King.

But when the King saw Umra-Singh, he looked at him narrowly, and knew him again, for all that he was changed. And he said to himself: Surely this is that very rogue, who came to me before to cheat me; and now, here he is again! And he said to Umra-Singh: I know thee, thou impostor. Beware! for this time thou shalt not escape. Then said Umra-Singh: King, be it as thou wilt. Only let me see thy daughter, and that quickly: for I have really seen that Lotus Land: thereafter deal with me as it may please thee best. And as he spoke, ungovernable impatience seized him: and he stamped his foot upon the ground, and tears came into his eyes, and suddenly he began to laugh. And the King looked at him with curiosity, and wondered at him: and he said to himself: Either this fellow is mad, or it is as he says, and he has really seen that Lotus Land. But he said again to Umra-Singh: Remember, if this time also thou art playing false, death is the reward. Umra-Singh said: Show me thy daughter, and put me then to any kind of death.

So the King sent for his daughter, and after a while, Shrí came in.

But when Umra-Singh saw her enter, he sobbed aloud, and strode towards her. And as she turned her eyes on him in fear, he plunged his fainting soul into their azure sea. And in an instant he forgot his journey and his toil, and obtained in that moment the nectar of emancipation from the hunger of longing, and the pain of separation, and the terror of untimely death. And Shrí looked at him, as he stood before her, and instantly she knew him again. And her heart beat in her bosom like a drum, and she was seized with trembling, and could not speak, for fear and doubt. For again the forgotten ties of her former birth fought for utterance in her soul, and yet she feared him for his insolence, and despised

63

him for his poverty: for he was ten times leaner and more ragged than before. And long she looked at him without speaking. And then at last she found her voice, and spoke, and said slowly: What! is it thou, most doughty traveller? And hast thou made another story? Good it had better be, thy second tale, for never shalt thou live to make a third.

But Umra-Singh leaned towards her, with hungry eyes, for his soul yearned for the repetition of a forgotten past. And he looked at her long and wistfully, till her glance quailed, for her spirit was mastered by his courage and his love. And twice he strove to speak, and twice he failed, while great tears fell from his eyes upon the ground. And then at last, he became master of himself. And he said: Dear, now use me as thou wilt, and put me to any death. But tell me first, before I die: How comes it that I see thee here alive, and yet I saw thee, in that Lotus City, lying dead upon a couch, in the cold rays of the moon?

Then Shrí threw up her arms with a shriek. And she cried out: Ha! it is the truth: this man has really seen the Land of the Lotus of the Sun. And suddenly, the veil of oblivion was drawn for an instant, and she caught a glimpse of her former birth, and knew her husband again. And instantly she ran to him, and threw herself into his arms, and hung on his breast, and clung to him, like a jasmine creeper on a noble tree. And tears fell from her eyes like rain, and she laughed for joy, and caressed his face with her hand, and said: Brave heart, and didst thou dare to go alone to that distant Lotus Land? Thou art indeed my own husband, in this life as in the last. And now, after long separation, I have found thee for an instant, and thou hast me. Only seek as well again, and we shall meet once more, and taste yet another drop of the nectar of mutual enjoyment, before we die: for so it is decreed. I say, remember: we shall meet again.

Then she stood up, and pushed him back, so violently, that he nearly fell. And all they that stood by watched her and wondered.

For as they gazed, she grew in beauty, like a waxing moon, and flashed like a great jewel, and dazzled the eyes of all like the brightness of a lamp: and the colour of her wondrous eyes shot from them and streamed about the room, and lit up its walls with glory like that of a setting sun. And seeing it, the King her father was full of joy, for he thought: Now she is going to be married, and I have attained the fruit of my birth. But the astrologers looked at each other in dismay, for they knew that she was about to die. So as they gazed, suddenly she drooped and fell, and lay before them on the floor, like a lotus smitten by the frost.

Then the astrologers said, gloomily: She has abandoned the body, and gone somewhere else. And the King, seeing her fall, and hearing them speak, lost his senses, and fell down beside her in a swoon. But Umra-Singh turned, and left the palace, and went out into the street.

X. Separation

And he reeled about like a drunken man, this way and that way, jostling the people, who marvelled and mocked at him: See, see, the ragged Rajpoot, the suitor of the King's daughter, whose very sight has killed her! But he heard nothing but the words of Shrí, and saw nothing but her eyes. And he staggered on, like a woo en doll, on feet that moved of their own accord, till as before he reached the tank, and sank down upon the ground, knowing neither where he was nor what he did, puzzled about the quarters of the world[67]. And like a man, out of whose universe the sun and moon and the five elements with their compounds have withdrawn, leaving him alone in the centre of empty space, he lay motionless, plunged in stupor, with dry eyes. Then all at once memory returned to him, and he began to weep. And he wept, as if he contained within him the very fountains of the salt sea, till at last from weariness and grief he fell asleep on the edge of the tank. And in his dreams Shrí stood beside him, and revived his parched soul with the nectar of her kindly glance, as a hermit's daughter refreshes with water the plants of the hermitage committed to her charge.

And after drinking deep draughts from those two fountains of pity and love, he awoke, and found that it was now night, and again he was alone at the moonlit tank. And he said to himself: Alas! alas! I found my bride, and lost her again at the same instant, through the terrible operation of sins committed in a former birth. Now indeed I am alone, for this time she is gone I know not where, and how am I to look for her? And yet she told me we should meet again, to keep me from despair. Therefore now I will wander away over the wide world, and spend my life in

---

[67] *dinmohita = desorienté.*

seeking her: for but this, nothing is left in life, and the hope of reunion is like the back of the Great Tortoise, my solitary refuge in the wreck of the three worlds.

So he rose up, and went out of the city, and wandered about, hither and thither, like a bubble on the waves of time. And he went from village to village, and from city to city, asking everywhere of all whom he met: Have you seen Shrí, my wife? you will know her by her eyes, for they are full of the colour of heaven. But however much he asked, he found no answer: nor could anyone tell him anything about her. On the contrary, all wondered at him and turned him to ridicule. And one would say: Who is this moon-struck vagabond who roams about looking for a blue-eyed beauty? And another: What wonder that Shrí has deserted such a ragged mendicant, who forsakes even the well-to-do! And others said: This distracted Rajpoot wants the moon, but he needs medicines[68]. And at last he abandoned altogether the dwellings of men, and wandered continually in the jungle, with no companions but his shadow and his sword, looking in vain for the path by which he had gone on his former journey to the Land of the Lotus, and gazing by day at the pools of blue lotuses, and by night at the heaven with its stars, for they were like mirrors and images of the hues and shadows of the eyes of Shrí.

---

[68] The point of these gibes depends on the various meanings of the word Shrí: which may mean his wife, or the goddess of fortune, or the moon: out of which come herbs or medicines.

XI. The Lord of the Beasts

Now in the meanwhile it happened that Maheshwara, as he roamed through the sky with Párwati on his breast, looked down to earth, and caught sight of Umra-Singh wandering in the forest, uttering lamentations, and exclaiming: O Shrí, where art thou hiding? Hast thou, like the desert, no pity for the antelope that is dying of thirst for the water of thine eyes [69]? And immediately he remembered his boon to Kamalamitra, and grasped the whole story from beginning to end. So he said to Umá with a smile: Go now to thy father[70], and wait for me: for there is here a matter that demands my attention. Then his consort said to him in a cajoling tone: What is the matter? tell me. Maheshwara said: I will tell thee afterwards: at present I have no leisure: depart. Thereupon the goddess went off pouting to the Snowy Mountain. But the moon-crested god descended to earth. And there, taking the form of an ascetic, he entered the forest. And standing in its densest part, his body white with ashes, garlanded with a necklace of skulls, with a half-moon in his yellow hair, he created by his supernatural power a gong, hanging from a banyan tree in the centre of the wood. And he struck with his trident a blow on that mind-born gong that resounded through the forest like thunder.

---

[69] There is here an untranslateable play on the word *mrigatrishná*, 'the thirst of the antelope,' i.e. the *mirage* of the desert, to which he compares her eyes.
[70] i.e. the Himálaya mountain, of which, or rather whom, Párwati is the daughter, as her name signifies.

Then instantly, hearing that terrible summons, all the denizens of the wood, Yakshas and Pishāchas, Rākshasas and Hamadryads, with the wild animals and the rest, assembled together and flew towards the sound, and crowded around the gong like flies or bees to honey or a dead body. And when they had mustered, they enquired humbly of that Lord of Creatures animate and inanimate: What orders has the Lord of All for his servants, and why are we now summoned? Then said the Great Ascetic: There is in this wood a lover looking for his bride. And she on her part will sometime or other be here to join him. See that none of you do them actual harm, by devouring or destroying them: for they are to work out their redemption in the wood, by the decree of destiny and my will and pleasure [71]. For they fell under a curse, and so became mortals: but when they meet here, and the circumstances are favourable, their curse will have an end. Therefore delude them if you will, but beware that you touch not a hair of their heads.

Thus he spoke, and all assented, prostrating themselves at his feet. And then he began to dance. Then all joined furiously in the festival of his favour, seized with the madness born of devotion, uttering ecstatic hymns of praise, each in his own language. So after that he had sported sufficiently, and bestowed on those adorers the nectar of his presence, that Lord whose left half is his wife remembered his promise to the Daughter of the Mountain, and returned to the snowy peak of Kailàs, to tell her the story and coax away her sulks.

---

[71] The Hindus never had a Lucian, to laugh at their mythological contradictions. They were always too much under the spell.

XII. The Other Body

But in the meanwhile Shrí, when she abandoned the body in Indirálayá, flew in the twinkling of an eye to the Land of the Lotus of the Sun. And there she entered that other body, lying in a couch in the Palace hall. Then instantly she opened her eyes, and rose up, as if awaking from a dream. And she was filled with astonishment, terror, and dismay, when she found herself alone in the empty hall. And she exclaimed: Alas! what is this mystery, and how came I into this deserted hall, and in which quarter of the world am I, and what has become of my husband? Now do I see the terrible consequences of sins committed in a former birth. Alas! how am I to regain him, and where is he to be found? Surely we are like two tiny fishes in the infinite ocean of time. Yet even so, despair is unavailing. Did not Sitá recover Ráma, and Shakuntalá, Dushyanta, and Damayanti cross the ocean of separation, and repose on the shore in the shape of the embraces of Nala? Truly omnipotent is the power of love, and what love was ever greater than mine? For it passes on from body to body, and draws fresh fire from each new birth.

Then she dressed herself in the white pall [72], and went hastily out of that empty palace, shrinking like a fawn at the echo of her own

---

[72] As this might sound bizarre to the English reader, accustomed to the elaborate toilettes of western ladies, he should know, that nothing can be more simple than the dress of a Hindu woman. A single long piece of stuff, wound like a petticoat round the waist, secured, and thrown over the head to form a

footsteps, and passed out of the gates, and ran through the deserted streets, down to the very edge of the sea. And there she stood with her bare feet lapped by the waves, looking out eagerly over the sea, with eyes that laughed at and shamed it of its blue. And it rose in agitation at her beauty, as if stirred by the moon, while the wind kissed her unaware, and played with her hair and clothes. Then she said: O Ocean, art thou too parted from someone, that thou heavest long drawn sighs? Art thou also wrenched with grief, that thou sprinklest me with the salt tears of thy spray?

And as she gazed, there appeared tossing on the waves a ship, like the realization of her desire to cross the ocean in visible form. Now that ship belonged to a great merchant captain, who was returning home from a trading voyage. And when he saw a female figure standing alone on the shore, he came quickly in a boat to take her captive. But when he got to the shore, and saw the wonderful beauty of her dark blue eyes and snow white raiment, he was struck with wonder, and became afraid. And he said to her in awe: Surely thou art some divinity, and no mere mortal maiden. Tell me thy name, that I may know whom to adore. Then said Shrí: Sir, I am no divinity, but a king's daughter; and I am seeking for my husband. Carry me, of your kindness, over the sea, for I must find my way to Indirálayá. But hearing this, that merchant was overjoyed; for he thought: Indirálayá is in another quarter of the world, and I will be her husband. For he was drowned in the ocean of her eyes. So he said to her: O thou true daughter of a King, my ship is thine and all that it contains. Come now, and I will carry thee whithersoever thou wilt. So Shrí consented. And the merchant in his delight counted the whole world as a straw, thinking he had got her for a wife. So when he got to the ship, he said to her: Truly this husband of thine is a sorry rascal. Out

---

veil, forms a garment that the Greeks might have envied. Nothing can surpass the taste, beauty, and grace of the way in which it follows and reveals without betraying the figure of its wearer.

upon him, who could leave such an incomparable beauty as thine to roam about the world without him! Forget him now, for I will be thy husband. Then said Shrí: This is impiety, nor is my husband to blame in this matter. Know, too, that to a good wife her husband is a deity. Then said the merchant: Thou shalt marry me whether thou wilt or not: and I care nothing for piety or impiety, but only for thy wonderful eyes. And now I have thee, I will keep thee. So he carried her in his ship, very carefully, closely guarded, to his own city, and shut her in an upper chamber of his house, hoping to prevail on her in course of time, neglecting his affairs.

Then Shrí said to herself: Alas for my beauty, which is a curse and no blessing to me, in that it has placed me in the power of this headstrong merchant! Nevertheless, even so, I have got over the sea. And now, I must lose no time in escaping from this infatuated sinner, or worse things may come about. And she went to the window and looked out. Now by the ordinance of fate it so happened, that at that moment the King of that city was passing by on his elephant. So when she saw it, Shrí said to herself: There is my deliverance in the form of an elephant. And now I must sin a little, to save myself from greater guilt. Then she called to the mahout: Come nearer, O driver of the elephant: for I am anxious to taste the delight of riding on an elephant. And hearing this, the mahout looked at the King. And the King looked at the face of Shrí. And Shrí shot at the King a blue glance from her eye. And instantly the King lost his senses, and said to the mahout: Do as she bids thee. So the mahout brought the elephant under the window, and Shrí let herself fall from the window on to his back. And she caught hold of the King to save herself from falling, and the King almost fainted from excess of joy, and the nectar of her touch. And without losing a moment, he carried her off to his palace, as delighted as if he had conquered the whole earth. But the merchant, when he found that she had gone, abandoned the body in his despair.

Then as soon as they reached the palace, the King said to Shrí: What is thy name and family? Shrí said: I am a King's daughter from a far country, and my name is Shrí. Then said the King: Thou didst well to forsake that miserable trader for me. Should the lioness, forsooth! Mate with the jackal? And now will I place thee, like a choice jewel, in the centre of my diadem, and thou shalt be the very apex of the summit of my fortune [73]. Then said Shrí: King, do not speak thus. For I am the wife of another. And I fled to thee for refuge, and not for frivolity: for yonder merchant would have made me his wife by force. So do me justice, and let me go: for I may not be a wife to thee.

Then said the King: Thy dark blue eyes have utterly destroyed my sense of right and wrong, which are now mere words without meaning, impotent to hold me as is a lotus stalk to fetter that elephant which brought thee hither; and in vain dost thou talk to me of letting thee go: thou askest me for my life: for till I saw those unfathomable blue lakes which thou hast stolen to make thee eyes, I never lived. Only consent, and I will efface by my devotion the memory of thy husband, as the sun dries up a shallow pool. But Shrí said: Say not pool, but ocean, on which the sun shines for ever, yet never makes it any less: for such is my love to my husband. But the King paid no heed to her words, which entered at his ear, but never reached his mind. For all his soul was in his eyes, feasting on the face of Shrí, which made him drunk like the juice of Soma [74].

Then seeing the state of the case, Shrí said to herself: Alas! I have escaped the lesser danger only to incur the greater, and become the prey of this unrighteous King. Now there is no help for me, save in stratagem, and the natural craft of woman. And she lifted up her lashes, and cast on the King a crooked glance, that almost

---

[73] He plays on her name. The old Hindu rajas had the same veneration for their royal fortune (*Shrí*) as the Romans for their *Fors Fortuna*.

[74] A play on her name, as a digit of the moon: Sonia is the moon, and the famous intoxicant of the early Hindus.

deprived him of his reason. And she said, moving her bow-arched eyebrows, with a smile: Out upon the heart of woman, for it is soft as a flower, and averse to constancy! Leave me awhile, for I must consider this matter. And yet, stay not away too long, for thou art good to look upon, and well-fitted to be my husband, were I not already the wife of another man. But hearing this, the King was utterly bewildered, and doubted the testimony of his ears. And he thought: Now she will consent, after a little coaxing. And he looked at her as she stood smiling at him, bowing like a flower from the weight of her bosom and the slenderness of her waist, and laughed in his intoxication, befooled by the roundness of her limbs and the blueness of her eyes, and forgetting that the Creator made woman to be an instrument of delusion, with an exterior of honey and an interior of poison. And he left her to perform his kingly duties, intending to return without delay, and thinking the fruit of his birth attained.

But as soon as he was gone, Shrí summoned a chamberlain, and said to him: Take me to the Head Queen, and lose not a moment, or it will be the worse for thee. And that chamberlain trembled and obeyed her, for he feared her power, saying to himself: The King would throw his kingdom into the sea for a glance from her eye, and now my life is on her forefinger. So when Shrí came before the Queen, she said to her: Lady, thou art my sole refuge. Know, that the King thy husband found me to-day in the city, and stole me away, seeking to make me his wife. Now contrive my escape, for I am the wife of another, and I may not be his wife. And do it very quickly, for this is an opportunity which will never occur again. Then the Queen looked at her, and said to herself: She says well, and I must indeed send her away without losing a moment. For if she remains here, and becomes his wife, the King will abandon everything for her sake, and the state will go to ruin. Moreover, he will never again have anything to do with me or any other of his queens: for her beauty is like a very feminine incarnation of the five arrows of the god of love.

So she summoned her confidential women; and they disguised Shrí as a dancing girl, and conveyed her secretly out of the palace without delay. But when the King returned, and found that she was gone, he became mad. And he put to death, of his retainers, everything that was male.

XIII. A Light in Darkness

But Shrí, when she got out of the palace, instantly went out of the city by unfrequented paths, and entered the Great Forest. For she said to herself: If I remain in the city, I may fall again into the power of the King, or, it may be, of someone still worse. For alas! every man that sees me is blinded by my eyes, and I shall not always find a door of escape from persecution. Moreover, to beauty without its guardian, wild beasts are less dangerous than men with souls through the influence of passion worse than those of beasts. Better far to be devoured by an animal, than become perforce the wife of another man.

So she went on through the forest for many days, supporting her life on roots and fruits and the water of the pools and streams. And she tore her clothes to pieces in the bushes, and pierced her feet with their thorns, leaving where she passed on the grass drops of blood, like rubies, mingled with the pearls of her tears that fell beside them, as often as she thought of her absent husband. And the deeper she went into the wood, the more her spirit sank, and the more her soul longed for the nectar of her husband's arms. Alas! the courage of women is but a pale and lunar image in the mirror of that of men, and vanishes in their absence. And at last there came a day when she was seized with panic, and a fear of unknown evil: and she sank down at the foot of a tree, and watered its roots with her tears.

Now it happened, that some Bhillas, hunting, by the decree of destiny, in the forest, came upon her track, and saw the drops of blood upon the leaves. And they followed them up, saying to themselves: Some wounded animal has passed this way. So as they came along, every now and then they stopped and listened. And suddenly, they heard the sound of the voice of a woman, weeping in the wood. Then full of astonishment, they proceeded in the direction of the sound: and all at once they saw Shrí, sitting under a tree, looking like an in-carnation of Rati grieving for her husband, when burned by Maheshwara. For her clothes were torn, and her hair was dishevelled, and her great eyes filled with tears resembled the petals of a blue lotus sparkling with drops of water cast upon them by the sporting of swans in a pool. So those wild Bhillas wondered when they saw her, and said to each other: What is this marvel of a dancing girl, so ragged and so beautiful, weeping alone in the wood? And then they went up to her and stood round her in a ring. And she looked in the midst of those black barbarians like a digit of the moon in the jaws of Ráhu. Then after a while the spell of her beauty entered and poisoned the hearts of those Bhillas, like one of their own arrows. And each one said secretly to himself: She shall be my wife. So they debated about her, and proposed to each other to draw lots for her. But they could not agree about it, and fell to quarrelling, and it was as if a stone had been dropped into a nest of serpents.

Then one laid hands upon her, and then another, till she was nearly torn in pieces. And finally they came to blows, and fought for her over her body, filled by the frenzy begotten by her beauty, and the desire of exclusive possession[75]. And very soon they were all either dead or dying of wounds, for each was more eager to destroy another than to protect himself: and they lay all about her unable to move. Then Shrí, seizing her opportunity, and urged by terror, rose up and fled away from them, being sprinkled by their blood, mingled with her own, for she had received in the struggle a blow from a Bhilla that was meant for another. And she ran on, stumbling over roots and creepers in her haste, till she came at last

---

[75] *ahamahamiká,* 'each one saying I, I.'

77

to a forest pool. And there she lay down at the edge of the water and drank greedily; and afterwards washed her wound and stains, and bathed her feet, and overcome by weariness, fell asleep. Then the moon rose, and stole through the trees and kissed her with beams that trembled with admiration[76]; and the wild animals came down, one by one, to drink at the pool, and obedient to the commands of Triambaka, did her no harm, but licked her feet and hands as she lay.

Now, as fate would have it, this was the very pool, at which Umra-Singh had met with Ulupí, the daughter of the Daitya. And in course of the night, Ulupí came herself to the pool, to dance and sport according to her wont. And when she arrived, she saw Shrí., lying asleep by the pool. So she came and stood over her, and marvelled at the beauty of her limbs, even though her eyes were shut. And at last, out of curiosity, she touched her on the bosom with her finger, saying to herself: Is this an illusion, or is it a real woman, and is she dead or alive? But Shrí shuddered at her touch, for it suggested evil to her sleeping soul. And she opened her eyes, and their deep blue awoke the envy of the daughter of the Daitya, and astonished her even more than before.

Then they looked at each other, like light and darkness, and each wondered at the loveliness of the other, forgetful of her own. And at last Ulupí said: Who art thou, and what is thy name and family, and whence past thou come to my pool, and why? Shrí said: I am a King's daughter, looking for my husband, whom I lost, by the operation of crimes in a former birth, at the very moment that I found him again, after that he had returned to me from the Land of the Lotus of the Sun. But when Ulupí heard her, she was filled with sudden rage and malice. And she said to herself: Ha! so this is that absent lotus of the day, by reason of whom my beauty was scorned, and set at nought by the handsome stranger who saw me dancing by my pool. And instantly she started up, and assuming a

---

[76] The Moon proper, in Sanskrit, is *Lunus*, not *Luna*.

terrific form, she gnashed at Shrí with teeth like saws, and made horrible grimaces at her, saying: Wretch, thou shalt never quit this wood, but wander for ever with thy accursed beauty among its trees, haunted and beset by hideous illusions till thou shalt long for death. Let thy absent husband save thee if he can. And she vanished with a peal of laughter, leaving Shrí fainting by the pool.

But Ulupí flew through the wood, and found Nightwalker, the old Wairágí, and told him all, and begged of him a boon, saying: Torment this miserable mortal woman, and deceive her with illusions for she has done me deadly injury. And Nightwalker rejoiced at the opportunity, for he remembered how Umra-Singh had defied him, and cut off his tongue in the wood. But he said: This is no easy matter, for we are forbidden by Pashupati to do her harm. But though I will do her no injury, I will delude this wandering wife of a vile husband, till she will desire to abandon the body of her own accord.

XIV. Illusion

But Shrí, when she came to herself, sat weeping, and fearing for
herself in the future: for she foreboded evil from the malicious
pranks of the daughter of the Daitya. And yet she could not tell,
how she could possibly have offended her, or deserved her anger.
And as soon as day broke, she rose up, and began to go trembling
through the wood, in which the shadows of night still hung
among the trees, starting at the noise of the falling leaves, and
yearning for emancipation from danger in the form of her
husband's presence.

Then after a while, she stopped and listened: for she heard among
the trees steps, as of one coming in her direction. And her heart
beat violently, as if to say: Let me abandon thy body, and so
escape the danger coming on thee. So she hid herself in a hollow
tree, and peeped out in terror. And suddenly, strange! there in the
dim twilight she saw her husband coming towards her, looking
just as he did, when she left him in the palace at Indirálayá. And
instantly she ran towards him, overcome by emotion and great
surprise, and caught him in her arms, exclaiming: At last, at last, I
have found thee again. And she wept aloud, and forgot in that
moment all her sorrow; and she looked at him, and laughed for
joy, and closed her eyes, as if, like the sun, the sight of him
dimmed and overcame the faculty of vision. Then after a while,
she opened them again, and started and shrieked, and her blood
became ice, and her heart stopped. For he that held her in his

arms was not her husband, but a hairy thing with hideous eyes, that resembled an incarnation of the brute in human shape; and it fastened those fearful eyes upon her own, and laughed and whined and panted like a beast with hot quick breath into her face. Then her senses abandoned her, like cowards, and she sank down to the earth in a swoon.

And when at length she revived, she looked, and saw that the sun was declining in the western quarter. But the moon had not yet risen, for it was the beginning of the dark half of the month. Then all at once memory came back to her, and she shook with agitation. And she said to herself: Was it a reality, or was it only an evil dream? Surely it was but a dream; for I am very weak and tired. And even now I cannot tell, whether I wake or sleep.

So she sat with her eyes closed; fearing to open them, lest she should see she knew not what among the shadows of the trees. And then the waning moon rose, and poured through the interstices of the leaves beams faint and pallid, as if sharing her own terror. And at last, unable to endure any longer the silence and the solitude, she rose up and began to move slowly, with hesitating steps, through the dark wood, not knowing where to go, yet not daring to stay where she was.

And suddenly, as she went, she looked before her, and there, in an open space, again she saw her husband, lying still under a tree. Instantly she stopped, and stood, balanced in the swing of vacillation. For the joy of reunion, and the desire of safety, and the fear of solitude drew her towards him like a threefold cord: while the memory of her deception, and the fear of illusion, and the anticipation of unknown danger, fixed her to the ground like roots. And she wavered and swayed on her feet, like a young shoot fanned by opposing breezes: while large tears fell from her eyes, like drops of camphor from a moonstone [77]. And as she stood there doubting whether he were dead or alive, for his face was wan in the light of the pallid moon, his eyes opened, and met her own. And he sprang up, and ran towards her, while she remained unable to stir, and took her in his arms, while she shrank from his embrace. And he exclaimed: The sight of thee has lifted me out of the mouth of death, for I had determined to abandon the body. And then he said again: Alas! and why, O thou of the lovely eyes, dost thou shrink from me? But Shrí remained silent, torn by suspicion, and shaken by the beating of her own heart. And ever and anon she raised her eyes, and looked at him in doubt. And then at last she said slowly: Art thou indeed my husband? is it really thyself and no one else? Then he said: What is thy question or thy doubt? Hast thou forgotten me already? Surely it is but a little while since I lost thee in the palace of Indirálayá. Then said Shrí, sighing: There came to me but now one who resembled thee in every feature, and deceived me: and even now, I shudder when I think of it, lest thou too should be another such as he.

Then he said: Dear, thou art weak, and a dream has deceived thee: but this time, it is no dream. Know that I am none other than myself, and thou art with me. Let me dispel thy terror with a kiss. And he bent down, and she raised her face with a smile, saying to herself: It was nothing but a dream. But even as she touched his face, it changed, and became gigantic and misshapen, with a large tongue that hung out of lips that resembled those of a cow; and it broke out into loud laughter, and disappeared. But Shrí fell to the ground, as if menaced by the outstretched forefinger of death.

---

[77] The Hindus have a superstition, illustrated in a previous page, that moonstones in the rays of the moon distil a sort of lunar syrup, nectar or camphor, supposed to be composed of the substance of the moon.

XV. The Dead of Night

So she lay, all night long: and when at length the day dawned, she came, though with difficulty, back to herself. And she tried to rise, but could not, for her limbs refused to do their duty. So she lay there, cold as snow, and shivering like the surface of a lake ruffled by the wind.

Then gradually the sun left his home in the eastern mountain, and ascended the sky. And warmed by his beams, a little of her strength returned: and after a while, she rose to her feet, which wandered away, and carried her where they would, until they brought her to another forest pool. And there she lay down, and leaned and drank of its water. And she looked into its mirror, and saw herself, slender and emaciated as the old moon, but pale and colourless as that moon at mid-day [78] And her long hair fell down over her shoulder into the water. Then she bound up that wet hair into a knot, and remained all day by the pool, not endeavouring to go further: for she said to herself: Rather let me stay here to perish of hunger, or furnish myself food to some wild beast, than continue my journey through a wood filled with illusions worse than a hundred deaths. For they wear the guise of a friend, and so finding entrance into my heart sting it like

---

[78] The same idea is beautifully put by Butler in Hudibras, where he calls the sun's light on the moon a

> Mysterious veil, of brightness made,
> That's both her lustre and her shade.

serpents, turning into poison the nectar of him whom most of all I long to see. Surely my sins in a former birth were terrible in their enormity: for I have suffered in this existence pain sufficient for many lives. And now I feel that I cannot long endure, for my strength is becoming exhausted. O that I could indeed find my husband, were it only to die in his arms!

So she sat by the pool, grieving like a female *chakrawáka* for her mate, while the sun made, like the enemy of Bali, but three steps over the sky. And when at last he sank, she also grew weary, and fell asleep on the edge of the pool. And in her dreams she saw her husband, and drank her fill of the nectar of his embraces. And then, in the dead of night, she awoke, and sat up, and looked, and lo! there in the moonlight she saw him again, silently sitting beside her. And she leaped to her feet in agony, and turned to fly, and screamed aloud. For there stood before her another husband on the other side. Then suddenly the whole wood was full of laughter. And her reason fled, and she became mad. And she exclaimed: Out on this wood, for it is full of husbands! And she began to run through the wood, shutting her eyes, and stopping her ears,

XVI. Before Dawn

And now, by the decree of destiny, it so happened, that Umra-Singh, having wandered through the whole world looking for his wife, roaming up and down in the forest, was lying asleep in another place, close to that very pool. And suddenly he laughed in

84

his sleep. For in his dreams he had found again the Land of the Lotus of the Sun. And he stood once more in the moonlit hall, beside the golden couch. Then slowly, slowly, he raised the pall, and looked long at the face of Shrí. But as he gazed, it became apeish, and stuck out at him a large red tongue. And he saw before him, not Shrí, but the old Wairágí. Then a shout of laughter rang in his ears, mingled with the voices of criers and the din of drums; and he started to his feet awake, with an icy sweat on his brow.

And as he stood there, doubting still, for the laughter in his waking ears, whether he woke or slept, he looked before him, and saw in the moon-light the figure of a woman, running towards him: and instantly he knew her to be Shrí. For out of the shadow of her floating hair her great eyes glittered in the moon like the blade of his own sword, and flashed into the night before her like lightning from a dark blue cloud. And he ran to meet her with a shout of joy. But Shrí, when she saw him coming, stopped short, and began to laugh like one possessed by a vampire. And crying: What, another! she turned and fled away from him faster than ever, covering her eyes with her hands. But Umra-Singh was so astonished, that he stood like a tree, rooted to the ground: saying to himself: Is it reality, or is it a dream? Yonder she flies from me in terror as if I were an enemy.

And then, seized with frenzy, he began to pursue her, calling aloud: Shrí! Shrí! So they ran through the wood in the moonlight, in and out of the trees, like a spotted panther and a black antelope. And suddenly, Shrí slipped and fell. And a tawny lion leaped out of the wood, before the eyes of Umra-Singh, and stood over her as she lay. Then Umra-Singh turned white with fear, and uttered a groan. And in a moment he reached them as he ran, and struck at the lion, with all his force, a blow of his sword. Then lo! that phantom lion vanished, for he was but an illusion of the crafty Nightwalker. But the sword fell, sharp and true, on the shoulder of Shrí, and cut through to her heart.

85

Then Umra-Singh fell on his knees beside her with a wail, and took his darling in his arms, while her blood gushed out over him like a river, carrying away her life. And as his hot tears fell on her face like rain, Shrí opened her dying eyes: and instantly they were full of peace, for she knew that it was her husband at last. And she said slowly: Weep not for me, O my lord, for I have attained the emancipation of union with thee. All day long, I have sought thee: but I have found thee in the evening, before my sun goes down: that is enough.

DAWN

AND at that very moment, the curse came to an end. Then those two erring lovers regained their immortal natures. And they looked at one another, dazed and bewildered, for they thought that they had awoken from a dream. And their spirits rose out of those mortal bodies which they had abandoned, and soared away to their heavenly home, locked in each other's arms.

But Maheshwara, from his seat on Kailás, saw them go. And perceiving all, by the power of his mystical intuition, he said to himself: There are those two foolish lovers rejoicing to have awoken from a dream; not knowing that it was but a dream within a dream, and that they are still asleep. And he laughed aloud: and the thunder of the shout of his laughter rolled and reverberated, and rattled in the blue hollows of Himálaya, like the sound of a drum.

www.ingramcontent.com/pod-product-compliance
Lightning Source LLC
Chambersburg PA
CBHW071745090426
42738CB00011B/2577